1826 Plan of Bristol by Donne

KINGSDOWN

Bristol's Vertical Suburb

Detail from T.L.S. Rowbotham's panorama 'View south from Kingsdown', 1830.

KINGSDOWN
Bristol's Vertical Suburb

PENNY MELLOR

and

MARY WRIGHT

PHILLIMORE

2009

Published by
PHILLIMORE & CO. LTD
Chichester, West Sussex, England
www.phillimore.co.uk
www.thehistorypress.co.uk

ISBN 978-1-86077-601-4

Printed and bound in Malta

Contents

List of Illustrations

Frontispiece: View south from Kingsdown Parade.

Preface

'Kingsdown ... England's only vertical suburb ... Nowhere else [in Britain] is there an 18th-century suburb apparently hanging in mid-air over a big city,' wrote Ian Nairn, the architectural critic, in the *Observer* in the late 1950s, when the terraces on the slopes and summit of the King's Down were under threat of demolition by the authorities. John Betjeman, too, added his support to the vigorous and concerted opposition of the Kingsdown residents and local and national organisations: 'This airy suburb, this place of Georgian view, commanding terraces, trees, cobbled streets, garden walls and residential quiet ... all the more attractive for its unexpectedness so near the middle of Bristol.'

Today, Kingsdown is less threatened, and indeed is a thriving community, as demonstrated in the support and encouragement we have received while researching this book. We are in particular most grateful to the many house owners who have allowed us to consult their property deeds and to the invaluable recollections of residents past and present.

We also wish to thank those institutions and individuals who provided illustrations and gave permission for their publication, in particular: Blaise Castle House Museum (image 12); Chris Brisley (image 55); the Bristol Museum and Art Gallery (images 3, 9-10, 24, 34, 44-5); the Bristol Record Office (images 4, ref. 17563/1 fol. 129, and 50); the Bristol Reference Library (image 6); the Bristol Region Building Record at the University of Bath (image 59); Gerry Brooks, editor of *Bristol Times*; Bristol News and Media (images 49, 60-3, 65-6, 68, 72); Llewellin's Gears Ltd (image 47); Loxton Collection, Bristol Central Library (images 16, 38, 48); Stephen Macfarlane for access to his High Kingsdown and other archives; David Mellor for his drawings of the Down's development through the centuries and his photography; Michael Tozer for several pictures from his collection (images 36, 52, 56); Alan Turton for his drawing of Civil War fortifications (image 7); and John Winstone for a photograph from the Reece Winstone Archive (image 37). We are also indebted to the late Amy Geaney for her invaluable file of press cuttings of the 1950s and '60s (images 60-3).

Oh what a Prospect!

by Julia Donaldson & Alison Smith

KINGSDOWN
250
1737 1987

Sign: 16th century

The Kingsdown field where once the King's men jousted
A medieval priory there stands,
But now King Hal commands the monks be ousted;
The priory's on sale as house and lands,
    Oh what a prospect!
    All for to swell the royal revenue
    But what a prospect! At least there's still a fine commanding view.

Sign: 17th century

A civil war breaks out, alas, and Bristol
Is bound to be besieged, unhappy port.
Our pleasing manor's meads will ring with pistol;
On Nine Tree Hill they're putting up a fort.
    Oh what a prospect!
    Farewell to peace; tranquillity adieu.
    But what a prospect! At least there's still a fine commanding view.

Sign: 18th century

Worse horrors yet! The city's overcrowded,
Each prosperous pedlar wants his country plot.
Fair Kingsdown's air with smoke will soon be clouded;
A building site will ruin a beauty spot.
    Oh what a prospect!
    Railings and bricks where once the green grass grew.
    But what a prospect! At least there's still a fine commanding view.

KINGSDOWN
250
1737 1987

Sign: 19th century

Our houses with their pediments and pillars
No longer seem to draw a wealthy breed.
Victorians prefer large Cotham villas;
Kingsdown, they say, is slowly going to seed.
  Oh what a prospect!
  In our decline we mourn the well-to-do.
  But what a prospect! At least there's still a fine commanding view.

Sign: 20th century

And now the Council, shocked by our condition,
Sets out to finish what the blitz began.
Streets not already felled face demolition,
And flats rise up to realise the plan.
  Oh what a prospect!
  We like old houses, concrete is not us.
  But what a prospect! Although they blot out our fine commanding view.

Sign: And now?

Thanks to the residents and their campaigning
The executioner has stayed his hand.
Our terraces, or those of them remaining,
Are loved, repaired, restored, allowed to stand.
  Oh what a prospect!
  And every year we'll celebrate anew.
  Yes what a prospect! Come and enjoy our fine commanding view!

Introduction

The King's Down, on which the Georgian suburb of Kingsdown was built, rises steeply some 250 feet, half a mile to the north of Bristol city centre. From its summit, looking across the city and the Avon valley, can be seen the heights of Lansdowne to the east and of Dundry to the west.

Over the centuries the Down has had a rich and varied history, its development intimately linked with that of Bristol, and this is its story from early times to the present day. It is a story of contrasts: from peaceful pastures to fiercely defended Civil War fortifications; from favoured meadows, for citizens of the smoky Georgian city to stroll and play in, to a hillside covered in terraced houses reflecting the fashionable architecture of the day; from elegant streets to blitzed inner-city dereliction; and from threats to its very existence to today's secure community. It is a story of Kingsdown's streets and spaces, its developers and its residents.

From medieval times the King's Down was a part of the land of the Priory of St James and the post-Dissolution disposal of this land was key to its subsequent development. Meantime the fortifications built on the summit were to play a key role in both Royalist and Parliamentarian battles to take the city of Bristol. In the early 18th century Kingsdown became Bristol's first Georgian suburb. 'Garden houses' were built on the slopes for wealthy merchants and by the middle of the century plans had been prepared for a formal layout of terraces on the contours, maximising the panoramic views and linked by distinctive steep-stepped lanes rising up the hill. The houses displayed a spectrum of Georgian domestic architecture from the informality of the early 18th century to the planned regularity fashionable by the end of the century.

In Victorian times, as Bristol's outer suburbs proliferated, the area became less fashionable. The authorities installed necessary services, but by the end of the century the houses of Kingsdown had become increasingly shabby and derelict. By the 20th century the terraces were under severe threat, at first by the bombs of Hitler's blitz of Bristol, then by post-war planning for a brave new world, with zones allocated for expansion of the university, hospital, and public housing. The fight for the Kingsdown terraces made headlines both locally and nationally for many years as residents and well-wishers challenged the authorities, winning some battles, losing others. Though many houses were lost, sufficient survived to enable Kingsdown slowly to revive and become the strong neighbourhood it is today.

1   *Victorian OS Map showing, superimposed, the medieval field boundaries of the King's Down.*
   - ***Lower Montagues*** *includes the area north of Montague Street now occupied by hospital buildings*
   - ***Upper Montagues*** *runs northwards from it up to and including the west end of Kingsdown Parade and from Alfred Hill to west of Montague Hill*
   - ***Dove/Pigeon Croft*** *runs from King Square to Dove Street and also includes Hillgrove Street and Lower Gay Street*
   - ***Prior's Hill Close*** *is the land on which Somerset Street is built*
   - ***Kingsdown Mead*** *is the remainder of Kingsdown Parade*
   - ***3-Cornered Handkerchief*** *is around Southwell Street*
   - ***Green Close*** *contains the area later known as High Kingsdown: Paul Street, Salmon Street, Clarence Place, Oxford Street, Henrietta Street and Portland Street.*

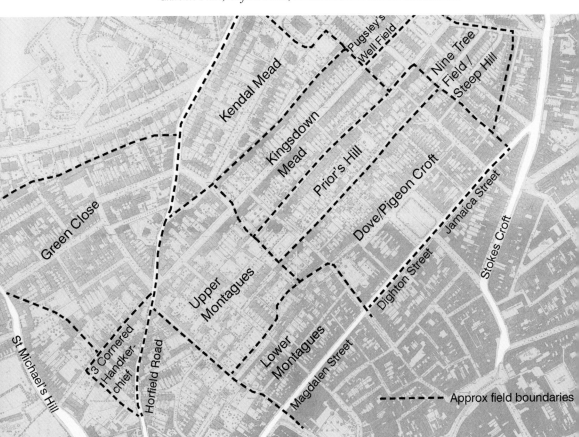

As any long-term resident of Kingsdown will bear witness, the boundaries of the area now called Kingsdown have varied over time and according to circumstances. In this account it is defined as the area on the slopes and summit of the King's Down. In medieval times this was the fields of the Lower Montagues north of Marlborough Street, Upper Montagues, Dove Croft, Prior's Hill, Kingsdown Mead and Green Close; today it is the area bounded by the line of Alfred Hill in the south-west, Kingsdown Parade in the north-west, Dighton Street in the south-east and Hillgrove Street in the north-east, together with the area immediately to the north-west now mainly covered by the houses of High Kingsdown.

However, because of the acknowledged historical ambiguity to the north-east, Pugsley's Well field and Nine Tree field, parts of present-day Cotham, are also included where it seems appropriate.

ONE
The King's Down

Romano-British and Medieval

The King's Down seems to have been little touched by human activity prior to Anglo-Saxon times, when the settlement of Brigstowe (later Bristol) was founded. Though other heights in the Bristol area were settled in the Stone or Iron Ages, there has been no pre-Roman evidence found of man's habitation on the King's Down, and only peripheral signs of activity during the centuries of Roman occupation.

To the immediate north of the King's Down, it is thought that the first-century road from Bath (*Aqua Sulis*), the Romans' main centre in the region, to Sea Mills (*Abona*), a small river port at the seaward end of the Avon Gorge, came to within half a mile of the Down before heading north-west. To the south, traces of a small Romano-British settlement of the second to fourth centuries were found close to Upper Maudlin Street during excavations there in 1973.[1] And on the King's Down itself, a coin of the Emperor Constantine (Emperor from 306 to 337) was in 1780 found buried at the west end of Kingsdown Parade, behind the then *Montague Inn*.[2] No other trace of Romano-British occupation has been found on the Down though, so it would seem that its summit was used only as a resting or vantage point for those early road travellers and settlers, to overlook the Avon valley or view the distant hills.

It was to be another 700 years, around the beginning of the 11th century, before medieval Bristol came into existence, sited at the lowest convenient bridging point of the river Avon. The Domesday survey of 1086 suggests that the town was already a flourishing settlement and by the beginning of the 12th century Bristol was a thriving fortified port, handling much of Britain's trade with Ireland.

The slopes and summit of the King's Down became simple meadows and pastures, providing hay and grazing for animals and open space for the citizens of the busy city below. The occasional lane climbed its steep slopes and early conduits conveyed its pure water down into the city for drinking and washing. One such conduit was excavated in 1973 and a fraction of it preserved below Upper Maudlin Street and Lewins Mead.[3] Apparently here it is a head-high tunnel with a channel in the bottom that would have held a lead pipe. Also found nearby was a second enormous conduit, in part some six feet wide and ten feet high with a narrow chamfered bottom, and it is thought this would have been a sewage drain, with a continuous flush provided by a ducted stream, prone to flooding, that again would have run down the Kingsdown slopes. It is easy to see how later stories arose of tunnels leading from the Georgian houses of Kingsdown, either for smuggling or safe passage to the city port below. The only building mentioned on the slopes of the King's Down in medieval documents, though, was a dovecot, housing a ready source of fresh meat. The residents of Bristol preferred to remain close to their work, living safely enclosed within the city's walls.

The plateau at the summit, however, may also have had another use during this period, one that would explain the name King's Down. The land is said to have been used as a jousting place for the king's soldiers, and an exercise ground for their horses, garrisoned at the 11th-century royal castle of Bristol. It is suggested that the troops would muster beneath the castle keep at the south end of Marshall Street,[4] now more or less modern-day Merchant Street, from where they would march in a direct line from the castle, across Broadmead and past St James's Priory to the King's Down. Documentary evidence for this is slight, but William of Worcestre, writing in 1480, mentions Marshall Street and refers to 'the road going [up] the steep hill of St James's Priory past the jousting place of olden days'.[5] Worcestre describes much of Bristol, his native city, in precise detail, recording for instance the exact number of 'steppys' or paces between one site and the next. Unfortunately he was not equally specific in his description of what is very probably Kingsdown.

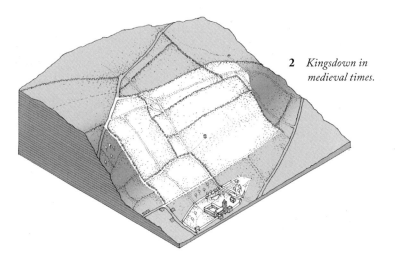

2 *Kingsdown in medieval times.*

The Down's earliest known documented history starts in the early 12th century when it became a part of the estate of St James's Priory, founded *c.*1129 by Robert, Earl of Gloucester, the illegitimate son of Henry I. The King, anxious to consolidate his disputed claim to the throne, needed reliable supporters in important places and Bristol was emerging as one of the most prosperous towns in the country. When Fitzhamon, his faithful Lord of Gloucester, died without male heir in 1107, Henry created his son, Robert, Earl of Gloucester, cementing the alliance by marrying him to Fitzhamon's daughter.

Robert completed his father-in-law's work of rebuilding Bristol Castle and, having taken on Fitzhamon's role as patron of the Benedictine monks at Tewkesbury Abbey, also founded a cell of that establishment in Bristol. This was St James's Priory, the first monastery in the city. It is said that one tenth of the stone Robert imported from Normandy to restore the castle was reserved by him to build the Priory's Lady Chapel,[6] probably the first building on the site.[7] The King had previously given his son several of the large estates that formed part of the Barton Regis, the royal farm estate to the north of the river Avon. Now, in order to ensure the Priory's future income, Robert, and later his son William, endowed the monks with major parts of the Barton lands—and these included the grazing fields on the King's Down.

William also entitled the monks in 1174 to the income from letting pitches at the annual fair held each year in the Horsefair, in front of the Priory. It was a lucrative source of wealth for the monks and indeed Bristol. St James's Fair, as it became known, grew into one of the greatest business gatherings in the kingdom, attended by merchants from all parts of the country and even from the continent. They came by day to barter, buy and sell, and by night to be entertained. The fair continued to be highly popular throughout the next six centuries, though by the 18th century it had become wholly hedonistic, a festival of pleasure, spectacle and performance with trade only in trinkets and sweetmeats. Later still, in the 19th century, the clergy and civic authorities—increasingly unhappy about the pickpockets, confidence tricksters, beggars and prostitutes there—succeeded, in 1838, in closing it down.

In 1374 it was decided that the population living around the Priory was sufficiently large to warrant the creation of its own parish, St James, and the monks' church was given the status of a parish church, probably regularising an arrangement whereby the local people previously attended mass there. Agreement was reached that the monks would provide the stones, and the parishioners the labour, for building a tower and belfry—with future profits from bell-ringing shared between them.

3 *St James's Fair, Samuel Colman, 1824. Here the fair is shown 13 years before it was closed down. The picture is well worth detailed examination at the City Museum, where the symbolism in the activities depicted is explained, from the perceived sinfulness to the campaign to abolish slavery.*

The parish boundaries, defined by the placing of stones, were beaten annually on Holy Thursday, the third day before Ascension Day, from late medieval times onwards. A procession of vestrymen and choirboys would perambulate, striking the stones. Planks were used to cross ditches and hedges were opened and closed. Sometimes, though not mentioned in the St James's account, the boys would also be struck to help them remember, though not seriously, for the perambulations, certainly by the middle of the 18th century, were a very jolly affair. In 1751 the St James's procession is described: it 'went in a little court belonging to houses occupied by Mr. Bath and Mr. Taylor, so through a back Kitchen or Wash house, behind said houses where there is a ladder put up at times of processioning and divers boys and others goes over the wall, by help of said ladder, into a garden'. From thence down the lane 'where there is a bough sticked up to tell we come to the crasse lane [Stokes Croft/Ninetree Hill junction], and so along … unto the place where the Boyes have Cakes and Ales as customary'. The vestry signed off the perambulation with 'and thence to dinner' at the *Full Moon* in Stokes Croft.[8]

The vestry (parish officers) were extremely rigorous about enforcing their parochial rights, a major source of their income. However, adjoining neighbours and developers were not, it would seem, always scrupulous in observing them: St James's parish is on record as issuing a stern warning to St Michael's, which had taken for itself 'two houses and rated them for King, Poor and other Rates'.

The establishment of St James's parish boundaries coincided with a redrawing of Bristol's own boundaries. In 1373, after receiving petitions from townsfolk and a payment of £400, Edward III granted a charter that raised Bristol to county status. Until then its boundaries had straddled the counties of Gloucestershire and Somerset, compelling Bristol residents to travel to Gloucester or Ilchester to settle legal disputes. The new boundaries of the City and County of Bristol were established by a perambulation undertaken by ten commissioners appointed by the king. These were to remain fixed for the next 450 years until the Municipal Reform Act of 1835.

To the north of the city the boundaries cut right across the Priory's fields. On the King's Down the lower half of the land was assigned to Bristol while the rest remained in Gloucestershire. This division was reflected in St James's parish boundaries, with the Bristol land designated the in-parish and the Gloucestershire land the out-parish.

Post-Reformation

In 1540, some four hundred relatively uneventful years after its founding, the life of the Priory at St James's came to an end, dissolved by order of Henry VIII as part of the Reformation. Four years earlier the Priory was, according to contemporary documents,[9] already down to only two 'religious men'; and in the previous year, probably anticipating seizure, the Prior of Tewkesbury Abbey had leased the Priory, its lands and its properties to a courtier named Sir Anthony Kingston. Dissolution came in January 1540—the oldest religious house in Bristol was the last in the city to surrender—and the Crown became holder of Kingston's 99-year lease to the Priory and its estate. Four years later Kingston assigned that lease to Henry Brayne, a London merchant tailor (though born in Gloucestershire) and major purchaser of Bristol monastic property. Brayne later purchased the freehold from the Crown for £667 7s. 6d.[10]

Brayne converted some of the monastic buildings to provide 'a capital mansion house or manor place' for himself and his family, which in his will of 1567 he still called St James. The monks' refectory became a great hall and their dormitory a long gallery, and the house is described as overlooking a 'great green court'—probably the grass of the one-time cloister. The nave of the monks' church, already parochial, survived Dissolution and continued as a parish church until the 1980s.

4   *The remains of the east end of St James's Priory church, looking north from the churchyard, from a drawing of c.1630. The building in the centre with the large doorway is the Lady Chapel and the crenellated walls and gatehouse to its right are thought to be the entrance of Henry Brayne's mansion house.*

Henry Brayne died in 1567 and his heir, his son Robert, two years later. Robert died childless and his will, in which he left his property provisionally to his wife, Goodith, provoked a family dispute, with his sister Ann challenging its validity on the grounds of Robert's insanity. She lost the case though, so Goodith retained her tenure, with Robert's sisters, Ann and Emilythys, as joint heiresses.

Both sisters had married well, Ann to Sir George Winter, the owner of Dyrham Park in Gloucestershire, and Emilythys to Sir Charles Somerset, son of the Earl of Worcester. The two husbands took control of the inheritance—women were not allowed at that time to hold land in their own right—and in 1579, following Goodith's remarriage, the two men drew up a Deed of Partition which listed all the Priory lands and buildings and apportioned them between the two families.[11]

Of fields on the King's Down the Winters took the Lower Montagues, which adjoined Brayne's mansion house, and contained a little pool and an orchard (now part covered by the coach station), the Upper Montagues to its north (stretching from Alfred Hill to west of Montague Hill and up the hill to Kingsdown Parade), and Kingsdown Mead, a close of pasture at the top of the hill, extending in length from the Upper Montagues on the west to Fremantle Square on the east (the land on which much of Kingsdown Parade is built). The Somersets' portion was Prior's Hill, running lengthways from the Upper Montagues to Fremantle Square and in breadth between the bottom of the gardens of Kingsdown Parade and the north side of Dove Street (the land on which Somerset Street is now built). They also owned the Harpe, Whorestone and Upper Barnsdall closes of meadow or pasture (later known as Pugsley's Well Field and Nine Tree Field - see p. xii) and Tophey 'in which stands a Culverhouse'. A culver is another name for a dove, hence the field's more common name of Dove Croft or in later deeds, more prosaically, Pigeon House Field. The 'capital Mansion house' of St James itself, the original Priory, was, as detailed in the 1579 deed, divided in half to provide two residences, for the Winter family to the west and the Somerset family to the east.

A generation later, in the early 17th century, living in former religious buildings was no longer fashionable and by the middle of the century the Priory site was almost unrecognisable. The mansion house had gone, replaced by buildings given over to industrial uses—a warehouse, a sugar house and a number of ancillary structures—and tenements, courts and cellars are shown on old plans of the site. Apart from the nave and tower of the parish church, there was nothing to recall the rich history of the Priory that had stood there for over 400 years.

The Civil War, 1642-6

Throughout the summer of 1642 England had been inching hesitantly, but inevitably, towards civil war. Those who took up arms cared passionately about both religious and constitutional matters, but it is probable that most of Bristol's population, caught between the extremes of the King's High Church supporters and the Parliamentary religious zealots, rejected both.

The city certainly took, and tried to maintain, a non-aligned stance. The members of the Common Council, the governing body of the city, were local merchants plying both large and small trades who were preoccupied with maintaining the conditions that would protect and promote the city's commerce. Bristol was a flourishing port, second only to London, with strong trading links to Ireland, France, Spain and Portugal. War, bringing the threat of disrupted trade, rising food prices and high taxation, was to be avoided at all costs. So while prudently strengthening the city's defences, its leaders were petitioning both King and Parliament to seek reconciliation.

It was not to be. Although the first major battle, at Edgehill in October 1642, ended indecisively, it only strengthened determination on both sides. In December that year Parliamentary troops entered and occupied Bristol, after which taxes and loans had to be raised to maintain the forces and improve the defences around the city against the expected Royalist attack.

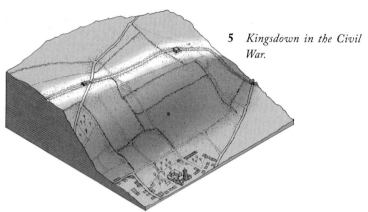

5   *Kingsdown in the Civil War.*

The northern defences, in which the King's Down was of prime importance, consisted of a continuous bank and ditch, linking five forts and smaller strong points (redoubts): the Water Fort by Hotwells Road, Brandon Hill Fort, Windmill Hill (later known as the Royal Fort) and, on the King's Down, Colston's (formerly Jones's) Fort and Prior's Hill Fort. From Prior's Hill the line of defences ran south-eastwards to the river Frome, before turning westwards to meet the river Avon. A Dutch engineer, Sir Bernard de Gomme, who was present at the first siege in 1643, wrote a detailed description of the line of these defences.[12] The rampart connecting the forts comprised a bank one and a half to two metres high and about a metre thick at the top. It was fronted by a ditch two metres wide and one and three-quarter metres deep, but that depth would increase to as much as three metres around the forts. As the historian John Lynch points out,[13] such an earthwork would present a considerable obstacle to assaulting infantry. A soldier at the bottom of the ditch would have faced an earthwork embankment about four to five metres high.

The location of both Kingsdown forts is known. Colston's Fort, often described as a redoubt, stood 'beside Alderman Jones's garden'[14] on the north-western side of what is now Montague Place and, according to Nicholls and Taylor, its earthwork ramparts continued north-east along the line of the lane now known as the Back of Kingsdown Parade.[15] Prior's Hill Fort, 25 metres square, stood near the south-western corner of what is now Fremantle Square. It was regarded by both sides in the Civil War as the key to the whole defensive line and, as such, was bitterly fought over in both sieges of Bristol.

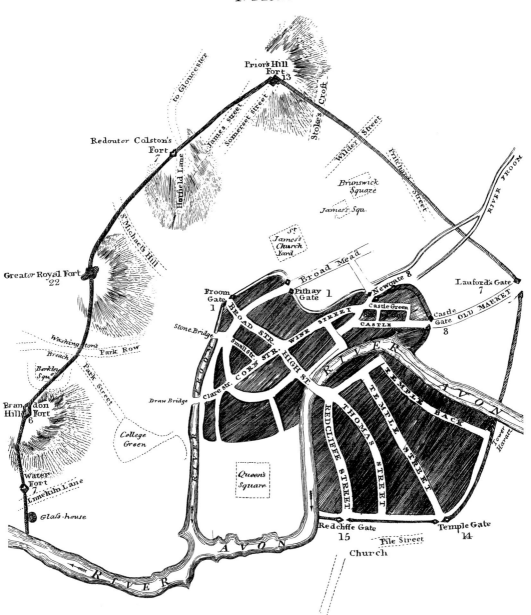

NORTH

SOUTH

6 *Sketch of the outworks of Bristol in 1644, Edmund Turner, 1801.*

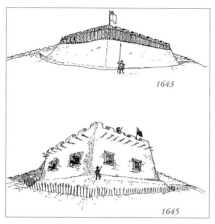

1643

1645

7   *Prior's Hill Fort. Reconstruction sketches of the 1643 and 1645 forts, drawn by Alan Turton.*

On 23 July 1643 the besieging Royalist forces under Prince Rupert, the King's cousin, moved into position. Lord Grandison was the commanding officer charged with launching the attack on Prior's Hill Fort and its sallyport, a substantially built high gate that completely blocked Stokes Croft. The Parliamentary commander defending Prior's Hill Fort was Captain Robert Blake, later Admiral Blake.

On the first day of battle the Royalist artillery was trained on Prior's Hill Fort in an attempt to weaken its resistance. Grandison then turned the fire on Stokes Croft gate, spending one and a half hours in a futile attempt to break through. Having failed there, he resumed the attack on the Fort. It did not appear to have been weakened by the previous day's bombardment, however, for time and time again Grandison's men were driven back by a hail of fire. Even when they advanced as far as the ditch they were unable to scale the great height because their ladders had failed to arrive—apparently because they had attacked ahead of schedule. Grandison, unwilling to give up, made another attempt to climb the sides using a ladder he had found nearby, but was shot in the leg, a wound that was eventually to prove fatal. His demoralised troops made their retreat.

The Royalists had then been driven back on every front. However, a breakthrough eventually came at Washington's Breach, near the present City Museum, where the defences were said to be incomplete. The attackers were reinforced by the contingent that had failed at Prior's Hill Fort. Realising that his force was now outnumbered, the commanding officer, Colonel Fiennes, sued for terms. Prince Rupert may have been relieved to see a way of ending the conflict, for his side had also suffered heavy casualties, and it suited the two commanders to agree adequate terms. Both sides had shown incompetence and poor discipline but, despite their inadequacies, the Royalists had achieved their end. Captain Richard Atkyns summed it up: 'When we were possessed of Bristol … I took the King's crown to be settled on his head again.'[16]

It is said that after this battle Prince Rupert threatened Blake with execution because he had continued to resist after the Parliamentarians had capitulated, but his excuse, apparently, was that Colonel Fiennes had forgotten to tell him to stop fighting.

Bristol remained in Royalist hands for the next two years, but by 1645 the military balance in the country was tilting in favour of the Parliamentary forces. In June the King was defeated at Naseby and the New Model

Army, under General Sir Thomas Fairfax and his Lt General Oliver Cromwell, advanced through the West Country taking one Royalist stronghold after another. Bristol was within their sights and Fairfax wanted to secure it before the Royalists could call up reinforcements from Wales and the south west. Prince Rupert, now Governor of Bristol, was confident that the city could withstand a general attack. It was well provisioned and, learning from the experience of inadequate preparation in 1643, the defences had been greatly strengthened.

Thomas Colston, a merchant, ardent Royalist and colonel of the local militia, had taken the initiative in improving the Kingsdown fort that was to be named after him. He enlarged it and increased its gun emplacements from two to seven (the costs re-imbursed by the Common Council), making it a more valuable link in the northern defensive line. Prior's Hill Fort was also rebuilt to make it a much more complex structure: the gun emplacements were increased from four to 13 with two tiers of loopholes. At the 1643 siege the northern forts had had a total of 15 guns; they had 55 by 1644. The ramparts of the forts were reinforced by projecting horizontal timber stakes called palisadoes and Cromwell, in his account of the 1645 siege, describes how his attacking pikemen balanced on these as they battled to take the fort.[17]

By 23 August 1645 Fairfax and Cromwell had advanced as far as Stapleton. They set up their headquarters at Stoke House and made a number of sallies into Bristol. On 2 September a Council of War was held at which the decision was taken to storm the city. The main thrust of the attack was to be on the line from Prior's Hill Fort to the river Frome. Four regiments were to cover both sides of Lawford's Gate (by Old Market), and five regiments were to focus on Prior's Hill Fort and the line running south-east.

This fort was again regarded as the key to the success of the operation and Rainsborough was ordered to storm it as 'the main business'.[18] Cromwell wrote later, 'Obtaining this strong fort, without which all the rest of the line to the Frome river would have done us little good and indeed, neither horse or foot would have stood in all that way, in any manner of security, had not the fort been taken.'[19]

Once it was agreed that Prior's Hill Fort was to be the main target, Fairfax and Cromwell moved their headquarters to a small farmhouse (later called Montpelier Farm) on Ashley Hill, which commanded a good view of the fort, and subsequently directed operations from there. A battery was thrown up beside the farmhouse to support the attack and at 1 a.m. on the morning of 10 September the signal was given by the firing of these guns and the lighting of a bonfire in the farmhouse garden. 'Immediately the storm began around the city and was terrible to the beholders,' wrote Sprigg.[20]

One regiment broke through at Lawford's Gate and advanced as far as the Castle Street gate. Another regiment of horses broke into the line around Prior's Hill Fort, but the defenders resisted their attacks. To the Parliamentary army Prior's Hill Fort appeared impregnable. Scaling its great height seemed impossible, for a ladder 'of 30 rounds' scarcely reached the top and even as they attempted the assault they were under constant fire from the cannon on the summit and the musketry from the portholes. The pikemen struggling to seek the top platform were especially vulnerable as they attempted to balance on the palisadoes.

Rainsborough later admitted that after three hours of fierce fighting he had come close to despair. There was, however, to be one final attempt. While Rainsborough's line extended from Ninetree Hill to Cotham, Colonel Hammond's regiment was backed up Arley Hill. It was decided that Hammond's men would make a dash down to Stokes Croft Gate and try to blast their way through it. They succeeded in opening up a gap wide enough for the cavalry to enter and drive the defenders back to the Barton, thus leaving a way clear to Prior's Hill through the Hillgrove. There they joined another force that had stormed in by the line at the Back of Kingsdown Parade. Together they entered the fort at the rear, weaker, side, creeping in at the portholes and then up the ladders to the top platform. Still the Royalist garrison would not admit defeat. They fought on, hand to hand, until forced to retreat to the lower, inner, rooms. There the exhausted and frustrated Parliamentary troops showed them no mercy. Most of the defenders were executed on the spot.

Fairfax and Cromwell, ensconced on Ashley Hill, watched the royal standard being hauled down from the top of the fort and as dawn was breaking they rode over from Montpelier to view the city from its parapets. Not that the firing had entirely ceased. While they were there a stray shot from the castle grazed the wall 'within two handbreadths of them'[21] and it is interesting to speculate what effect Cromwell's death in this moment of triumph would have had on the subsequent history of England.

Within hours of the loss of Prior's Hill Fort, Rupert surrendered the city. Fairfax gave Rupert very reasonable terms and the next day the flamboyant prince rode out from the Royal Fort, 'clad in scarlet, very richly laid in silver lace and mounted upon a very gallant black Barbary horse'.[22] For Bristol the fighting was over, and the following year, 1646, King Charles surrendered.

Post-war

At first conditions within the city walls were scarcely better than during the war. The city was still occupied by troops, it had been ravaged by the plague during 1644 and 1645 with the loss of 3,000 lives, and the coffers had been badly depleted by taxation. There had moreover been significant loss of revenue from the cancellation of St James's Fair in 1644, due to the 'distracted state of the country'.[23]

Slowly, however, over the following years, order returned. Eight years after hostilities ceased, in 1654, Cromwell felt sufficiently secure to order the demolition of Bristol Castle and it seems likely that the forts were slighted at the same time. The King's Down soon reverted to the pastoral peace of those 'closes of mead', 'meadows' and 'pastures' described in the early documents. Nevertheless, part of its defences may have remained intact for some years, for when James II visited the city in 1686 he rode up St Michael's Hill to 'review the line of defences from the Royal Fort to Prior's Hill Fort'.[24] Also Samuel Seyer, writing in the early 19th century, observed that although the greater part of Colston's Fort had been cut away by the [Horfield] road remainders could still be seen in a garden, and that the site of Prior's Hill Fort was still discernible though its exact form could not be traced.[25]

With peace came prosperity. The second half of the 17th century saw Bristol, well located in the west of the country, beginning to profit from its involvement in trade with the new colonies in North America and the West Indies. Ships from the port sailed out with manufactured goods, returning with tobacco, sugar and other goods for the home market. They also traded in labour to work on the plantations. At first Bristol was the main port of emigration for young English people going to work there, many kidnapped and taken against their will. By the 1660s, though, an increasing number of Bristol ships were trading in enslaved West Africans.

At around this time the Winters and the Somersets, Henry Brayne's heirs, began to sell off the Priory lands that they had inherited. In 1665/6 two closes of ground called the Montagues were sold by subsequent owners to Henry Dighton, a Bristol brewer, and though this sale is the only one that can be dated with certainty, Henry's will confirms that it was one of several transactions with him involving land on the King's Down.[26]

Henry Dighton came from a family of brewers established in Bristol since the early 17th century: parish records show that his father, Isaac, was leasing a house and orchard in Lewin's Mead from the board of trustees of St James as early as 1619.[27] Henry and his wife Katherine had at least six children: their surviving sons, George and William, followed the family tradition of brewing and their daughters married men within their social class, all described as gentlemen or merchants. The brewing connection appears to have been severed sometime in the 18th century as descendents followed diverse trades. They invested in sugar refining and from 1793 to 1824 members of the Dighton family, in partnership with others, operated from the Sugar House in Whitsun Court, beside St James's Church; one descendent was a tanner, another a haberdasher of hats. For many years the Dighton family retained local links: in 1775 Isaac Dighton lived in Montague Street, twenty years later his brother William was living, appropriately, in Dighton Street, and a George and Isaac Dighton were still collecting rents in Kingsdown in the 1860s.

When Henry died in 1673 he left his only surviving son, George, Pigeon House Close (seven acres of pasture), Brickhouse Close (eight acres of garden ground), and Prior's Hill Close (seven acres of pasture). To his wife, Katherine, he left The Montagues and a nearby paddock, formerly an orchard (together 16 acres), and the close of pasture called Kingsdown Mead (seven acres) with an adjacent paddock (one acre). Katherine in turn in 1677 bequeathed her inheritance in equal shares to her four daughters and their husbands.

The land inherited by Henry's son George also descended through the female line. When his sons died without issue the inheritance passed to the five daughters and their husbands. All had married into similarly prosperous manufacturing or trading families. One notable example was Ann Dighton, who, when she married George Bearpacker, a soap boiler from Wootton-under-Edge, united the interests of two families who had invested heavily in former Priory lands. The only daughter to retain and perpetuate the family name was Martha, who had married her cousin, a tanner named William Dighton.

The complications presented by this diversity of landownership were resolved by a series of agreements—the last of these in 1730—that established a good legal title in preparation for the sale of plots for development on the King's Down. (See Appendix: The Dighton Family, p. 97.)

TWO

From the King's Down to Kingsdown

The 18th century was a golden age for Bristol, with growth in both trade and industrial activity resulting in an increasingly affluent city. Its merchants continued to trade with the city's traditional overseas markets of Ireland, north-western Europe and the Baltics, and now they increasingly traded in goods and slaves with the West Indies and North America. By the beginning of the century Bristol was already the second largest port in the country after London, and though its national position had slipped by the end of the 1790s, the number of ships arriving annually from outside Britain had doubled and the tonnage carried quadrupled. Bristol was also the major industrial centre of the south west, much of it processing those traded goods. During this period both Fry's the chocolate makers and Wills the tobacco business started, and glasshouses, sugar-houses, distilleries, and shipbuilding yards proliferated. Its urban population as a consequence rose sharply from around 25,000 at the start of the century to around 69,000 at the end.

Even during the early years of the century, conditions within the medieval city were uncomfortable. As Daniel Defoe, visiting Bristol in 1724, observed: '[In] the City itself, there is hardly room to set another house in it; 'tis so close built.'[1] With the growth in population and with Bristol's merchants becoming increasingly prosperous and more sophisticated, expansion was inevitable and the city soon started to spread beyond its medieval bounds. Construction of Queen's Square began on drained marsh land in 1702, St James Square in 1707,[2] Orchard Street in 1716 and Dowry Square in 1720. The 1760s saw the beginning of the suburbs of Hotwells and St Paul's, and the 1780s the first terraces of Clifton and Montpelier. Bristol's earliest 18th-century Georgian suburb was, however, Kingsdown.

Semi-rural Kingsdown, 1700s-40s

Henry Dighton's grandchildren, quick to take advantage of this pressure for expansion, began to develop their inheritance, building on the Lower

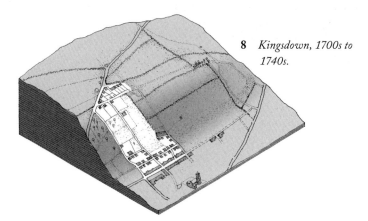

8   *Kingsdown, 1700s to 1740s.*

Montagues at the foot of the King's Down in the 1700s, and on the field to its north, the Upper Montagues, some thirty years later.

None of the earliest development, and indeed only some of the streets of the Lower Montagues, remains today, a result of the Bristol Royal Infirmary expansion. However, four of the 18th-century names there, Marlborough Street, Eugene Street, Blenheim Square and Marlborough Hill,[3] suggest a start date of development on the King's Down around 1704. In that year the English army under the Duke of Marlborough and Prince Eugene of Savoy, in close alliance, had won the Battle of Blenheim against the French and the Bavarians and there had been much popular acclaim. Certainly by 1710, on Millerd's updated map of that date, the western part of the field is shown covered by houses (the eastern part is covered by the map's entablature).

This development of the Lower Montagues was, however, effectively an extension of the city and some of the more affluent citizens began to look beyond for respite from urban smoke, smells and noise. Where better than the King's Down, described in *Felix Farley's Bristol Journal* as 'a perfect Terras, thrown up as it were by Art, for people to walk there and overlook the smoaky Town'.[4]

In the early 1730s the first plots on the Upper Montagues (the field on the western slopes and summit of the King's Down) were sold for house building by two of Henry Dighton's grandchildren, Henry Foot and his cousin Martha, and her husband John Still, and by the end of that decade construction was under way at the top half of Marlborough Hill and the western end of what was later to become Kingsdown Parade.

Early 18th-century Land Tax returns for the Upper Montagues indicate that most of these first Kingsdown residences were 'garden' or 'summer' houses, simple 'second homes' leased or owned by wealthy merchants. Roger Leech, specialist in Bristol's early domestic history, writes, 'In Bristol wealthy citizens with permanent residences in the

9 *Detail from Millerd's Map of Bristol, 1710. His map of 1673 was updated to show,* inter alia, *the Lower Montagues, the field immediately north of St James, covered in houses, and, on St Michael's Hill, Colston's Almshouses built in 1691.*

city centre had leased or owned gardens on the fringe of the city from at least the 15th century ... Gardens could serve as vegetable plots, retreats for tranquillity or pleasure, for weekends and holidays, for times of plague and pestilence, indeed for a whole variety of purposes, especially when provided with a small lodge, garden house or summer house.[5] These early buildings were detached 'cots' normally set in the corner of high-walled gardens. They were small—usually only one room on each floor—and of two or sometimes three storeys. Often they would be private, almost hidden from view as they turned their back on the street, looking inward across their gardens and from thence to the distant views.

Roque's map of 1742 seems to show two such houses set on the south side of Kingsdown Parade. The one to the west, set in a large landscaped garden, is almost certainly that of Giles Greville, a wealthy apothecary and early Kingsdown developer. The top section of the Upper Montagues, between Marlborough Hill and Alfred Hill and stretching as far as Horfield Road, had been sold in 1734/5 to Greville (the north-east) and Ralph Good, a goldsmith (the north-west portion), but in 1740 Giles Greville had consolidated his holdings by purchasing the north-west part from his neighbour.[6] The building to the east of Marlborough Hill, however, was initially not a summer house. The large plot on that side of the hill had been bought in 1737 by Alexander Stopford Catcott, headmaster of Bristol Grammar School, together with a house opposite, and the building was his stable.

Later in the 1750s, as the popularity of Kingsdown increased, the area began to be further developed. Greville built three further summer houses on his ornate gardens and Catcott's stable was converted to a small house.[7] Other summer or garden houses were built further down Marlborough Hill.[8]

The seven plots shown schematically along the north side of Kingsdown Parade in Roque's map were also probably built originally as second homes.[9] Certainly, the second of these was sold in 1733 to William Cooke, an ironmonger, for the construction of 'a summer house ... for quiet enjoyment free from incumbrances'.[10] The fifth is later described as a 'former summer house',[11] and from inspection it can be seen that both the sixth and the seventh show signs of having once been much smaller houses.[12] As people began to make Kingsdown their main place of residence these small houses were altered and enlarged. On the north side of the Parade the seven summer houses were extended to the edges of their sites and, often, other houses were built at the bottom of their gardens, all resulting in today's ragged terrace. Already by 1828, when Ashmead produced the first detailed map of the area, that early pattern on the north side of the Parade was difficult to see.

10 *Detail from Roque's Map of Bristol, 1742. In the centre west the Lower Montagues is shown completely built up and, above it, development has started on the Upper Montagues. In the centre are Tully's plans for the development of Dove Croft and Prior's Hill.*

11   *No. 6 Kingsdown Parade. A little-changed example of a summer or garden house at the west end of the Parade.*

At the south-west end of Kingsdown Parade and at the top of Marlborough Hill, however, the original form remains remarkably unchanged to this day. While the only 'garden house' left at its original size is that on the western corner of Marlborough Hill and no. 6 Kingsdown Parade,[13] its surviving neighbours are still detached and all clearly show signs of those much smaller original cots.[14] This cluster of four surviving houses provides us with a clear example of a form of early Georgian development that is rare in English cities today.

Of the two larger houses shown on the slopes in Rocque's 1742 map, only Marlborough House is still extant, though altered. This plot, two-thirds of the way up Marlborough Hill, was sold by Henry Foot and Martha Still to their cousins, David and Jane Jones, in 1737—and by 1741 the Joneses had built a house on the site. David's father, John, is elsewhere described as a 'mariner merchant', and a John Jones is prominent as a slave-vessel captain over these years, but it is a common enough name and it is difficult to corroborate whether slavery was a part source of their wealth. Nevertheless, the house the Joneses lived in was seen as an impressive one—described in a neighbour's deeds as 'a mansion' rather than the more usual 'messuage'.

Ralph Newham, whose substantial house is shown on the map to the south-west of the Jones's mansion is, to date, untraced. All that is

12   *Marlborough House. Drawing taken from an 1826 trade card for the Misses Jukes' Boarding School for Young Gentlemen.*

To be Lett,
And enter'd upon immediately,

THE DWELLING-HOUSE of the late M
Jane Jones, pleasantly situated on *Kings-Down-Hill* near
Newham's: Being a new, compleat, and well-finish'd Ho
with a very good Vault-Cellar, and convenient Offices; both Sor
Water, and a very pleasant Garden fronting the House.—☞ To be
with or without a Summer-House.
☞ For further Particulars, enquire of Felix Farley, at his P
ing-Office in *Small-street*.

13   *Marlborough House, 1752 advertisement (Felix Farle Bristol Journal). The phrase 'both sorts of water' refers to the h spring water that would have been used for cooking and drink and the soft rain water, stored in a large lead cistern by the sin in a reservoir beneath the floor, used for everything else.*

known is that Newham had purchased all the Upper Montagues to the south of the Greville land and that his house was valued for Land Tax at a higher rate than Marlborough House—more than keeping up with the Joneses.

On the summit of the hill Kingsdown's earliest inn, the *Montague*, stood at the far western end of the Parade, at the apex of the grassed triangle now known as Montague Green.[15] Built in 1737 on land also owned by Greville, and hence one of the earliest buildings in Kingsdown, the inn must initially have relied to a large extent on tradesmen from Horfield and the towns and villages to the north-east of Bristol coming into the city on business. Though there were some residents living nearby, in particular to the west in the parish of St Michael's, they would most likely have gone to the nearer, well-established *Green Dragon Inn* (now the *White Bear*) on St Michael's Hill.

However, the *Montague* would probably have been favoured by those enjoying the still untouched Kingsdown fields, whose popularity is described in a contemporary newspaper: 'Here the industrious Tradesman after breathing the impure Air of a close street, may sometimes retire and snuff the fragrant Gales … here the labouring Mechanick accompanied by his faithful Wife and little Pratlers take their Sunday's walk, or Summer Evenings' excursion.'[16]

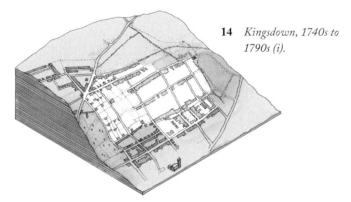

14   *Kingsdown, 1740s to 1790s (i).*

Suburban Kingsdown, 1740s-90s

The decades when development on the King's Down started in earnest were those when Bristol's trade with Africa and the West Indies was at its peak, with much of the city's wealth coming either directly or indirectly from the slave trade. Indeed, the second phase of Kingsdown development was initiated in the same year, 1737, that Bristol overtook London as England's prime slavery port.[17] Much of the money on which Kingsdown was built doubtless originated in that trade, whether through direct involvement in slavery or income gained through the slave plantations,

A SOLILOQUY *on* KINGSDOWN.

O! WHAT a wretched Chaos art thou made;
Once love'y KINGSDOWN! Nature's sweet Parade!
Once my Delight at Morn, and Evening Tide,
To breath thy healthy Air, and view thy Prospects wide,
No more on thee shall I my Sight regale
With the enchanting Views of *Avon*'s Vale:
No more from thee shall *Lansdown*'s Hill be seen;
Or *Dundry*'s, chequer'd o'er with Pastures green;
Or *Kingswood*, famous for her sable Wealth,
And scatter'd Cots the Rustic Seats of Health:
Or what's a nobler Scene than Hill or Dale,
Great BRISTOL seated in th' adjacent Vale:
No more from hence shall I her Tow'rs survey;
Her winding *Avon*, and her spacious *Kay*,
Where like a floating Wood her Vessels ride
Mounted aloft by *Neptune*'s flowing Tide.
No more on thee shall I these Scene's explore;
Thy Prospects spoil'd, thy Beauty is no more.
Deep Trenches now deform thy Walk, once fair,
And smoaky Lime kilns taint thy healthy Air:
Huge Heaps of Stones, and Mortar scab thy Brow,
For building Plebean Seats for nought but Show.
Each petty Tradesman here must have his Seat,
And vainly thinks thy Height will make him great:
But little Things look less the more they rise;
So Wrens may mount until they look like Flies.
Haste Brother e'er too late; and chose thy Spot,
Sell off thy Soot, and build thy *Kingsdown* Cot.
Come hither *Pedlars*, quit your dusty Stalls,
Here build your Seats, and rise your Garden Walls,
And when you've built it o'er—call't what you will,
'Twill not be KINGSDOWN then, but PEDLAR's Hill.

15   Felix Farley's Bristol Journal, *1765.*

provision of slave boats, or supply of trade goods for Africa—there is a long list of associated occupations.

During the 1740s-80s houses for the newly wealthy spread upwards and eastwards across the slopes of the Down in the fields of Dove Croft and Prior's Hill, and on the summit in Kingsdown Mead development of the field's western half spread eastwards during the same period. As a disgruntled poet of the time wrote in *Felix Farley's Bristol Journal*:[18]

> *O! What a wretched Chaos art thou made.*
> *Once lovely Kingsdown! …*
> *Deep trenches now deform thy walk, once fair*
> *And smoaky Lime kilns taint thy healthy Air.*
> *Huge heaps of Stones, and Mortar scab thy Brow*
> *For building Plebean seats for nought but Show.*

The development of Dove Croft and Prior's Hill, the two fields on the Down's slopes to the east of the Montagues, was to be in complete contrast to the almost contemporary semi-rural development of the Upper Montagues field.[19] In 1737 other Dighton heirs[20] commissioned the fashionable surveyor George Tully to draw up a much more ordered plan.[21] Tully had been responsible for the earlier laying out of Dowry Square within the city, but these fields were to be a planned suburb. Roque's 1742 map shows the plan Tully produced: King Square delineated with a double row of lime trees,[22] and the land at the foot and slope of the hill, up to and including Somerset Street, with named streets laid in a regular grid.

What the map cannot show is the steepness of the slopes and how the joining streets running at right angles (later to be known as Montague Hill, Spring Hill, Gay Street and Hillgrove Street)[23] are vertiginous. From Duke Street at the foot of the Down to Kingsdown Parade on the crest is a rise of 1:5, in parts even steeper. Spring Hill achieves this with a total of some 45 steps and is pedestrian only, while Gay Street had a similar number of pavement steps over only half the distance. Ashmead's map of 1828 illustrates how the detailed construction realised Tully's plan, with the streets on the slope of the Down developed in terraced form. The terraces of Kingsdown Parade, though not part of Tully's plan, continue his vision.

The overall layout of the terraces is significant. Somerset Street and Dove Street, together with those of the terraces on the south side of Kingsdown Parade, are set out with houses on the southern side of the street only, in order that they may take advantage of the slope to look over to the open fields of Dundry and the Lansdown hills. The houses on the north side of Kingsdown Parade, unable to see over the houses opposite, are, unusually, set at the back of their plots and formally entered through their gardens—the landscaping of those gardens serving in lieu of more distant views southwards. By the end of the century the Clifton terraces were to lift this *rus in urbe* philosophy to new heights; but here in Kingsdown is the first early move towards that picturesque ideal.

The realisation of Tully's scheme also clearly illustrates the contrast in mid-Georgian expectations between city and suburb. At the foot of the Down, and still feeling within the bounds of the city, the terraces of King Square are urbane in appearance, with houses of uniform façade design. Only eight of the 27 original houses have survived, but it seems likely all were originally of similar size and appearance. Michael Jenner,[24] the architectural historian, suggests their design may be by Thomas Paty, the established Bristol architect. Certainly an 'architectural' hand drew up their specification.

16   *The steep streets of Gay Street (left) and Spring Hill (right), 1912.*

In contrast, the houses of the terraces on the slopes above—Duke Street, Dove Street, Somerset Street (and, on the summit, the central part of Kingsdown Parade)—are of a much more varied style. In Georgian developments such as Kingsdown, it was the exception for an individual to buy a particular plot direct from the owner of the land for his own development and occupation. More usually a builder-developer would buy a piece of land and then lease out two, three, or even more, plots to smaller builders for the actual house construction. In the middle decades of the century those builders were then apparently free to construct houses according to perceived market demand, with a minimum of overall design control by the original developers.

It would seem that the builders of these Kingsdown streets anticipated the clients for this new suburb would be looking for something different from the uniformity of the urban terraced house. While the builders would have been seeking to maximise profit on their plots, they were usually building speculatively and therefore needed to reflect the aspirations of their would-be purchasers, the potential suburban resident of that period. In the place of uniformity they offered for some the freedom of expression that might be found in a country residence—albeit within the planning and financial benefits of the terraced form. These mid-Georgian terraces, consequently, reflect a motley of different house styles and architectural details, mixing the formal and the vernacular, grander houses being near neighbours of much more modest residences.

Though pairs or groups of houses would sometimes be almost identical externally, internally they were often very different.[25] For, once constructed, the houses would generally be offered for sale in a relatively unfinished state, the new owners having them finished and decorated to their own taste, either for themselves or, more commonly, for letting out.

In these early years of development, delays of up to twenty years between the sale of the site and actual building and occupancy were commonplace. Though the Dighton heirs tried to increase the value of their remaining assets by insisting in several of these early leases that building should commence within five to six years, the condition was frequently ignored. At that time it seems Bristol's merchants often favoured investment in land, not rents, seeing such investment as a safe repository for their money at a time when formal banking in Bristol was non-existent,[26] but as the prosperity of Bristol continued to increase in the second half of the 18th century so too did the popularity of this new suburb and the opportunities to realise their assets.

Building in King Square started in the 1740s and was largely complete by the 1760s,[27] and during the following decades new houses gradually covered the Kingsdown slopes. A contemporary writer complained:

Kingsdown, Delightful Spot! Is already begun to be dug up, and
to experience the rude deforming Labours of the delving Masons,
contaminated with the Itch of Building.[28]

On the Down's lower slopes in Dove Croft, Duke Street and Dove
Street—linked by Spring Hill, Gay Street and Hillgrove Street—were
the earliest of the hillside terraces to be developed. The major builder-
developer of this field was John Dalton, brick maker, who was granted the
land in 1738, and who then leased building plots to other local tradesmen
including, in particular, Robert Gay, mason. Both these developers are
still remembered today in Kingsdown in the names of Dalton Square
(below Dove Street South) and Lower Gay Street (between Jamaica
Street and Dove Street South). The name of a third developer, Joseph
Godwin, has proved more transient. The top of Montague Hill, called
Somerset Lane in 1760 deeds, was changed to Godwin Lane in deeds
of 1767, but in 1867 documents it is laboriously referred to as 'the street
formerly called Godwin Street, otherwise Prior Hill, afterwards called
Montague Street and now called Montague Hill'.

Duke Street and Dove Street were largely demolished in the 1960s
in order to build local authority flats, leaving little documentary trace
or evidence on the ground. However, photographs taken in the early
1960s illustrate a similar variety and form of houses to that seen today in
Somerset Street and Kingsdown Parade. Nineteenth-century maps show
Duke Street with terraced houses along its north-west side continuing

17 *King Square, south–west side.*

the line of the north-west face of King Square.[29] Dove Street has terraced houses at its south-west and south-east sides and two houses in the centre acting as a gateway to Spring Hill. In the centre of the street the long gardens of the King Square and Duke Street houses rise up the hill as far as Dove Street itself.

Immediately to the north-west of Duke and Dove Streets, a few houses were built on the western part of Prior's Hill Close in the late 1760s and 1770s. However, it was only after the sale of the greater part of that field in 1781 by two Dighton heirs that substantial development of Somerset Street started.[30] House building spread eastwards from Montague Hill and was completed over the following decade.

The 1775 Directory lists no residents in Somerset Street and that of 1785 only eight,[31] but most of the houses were occupied by the early 1790s. Then, as now, builders sometimes over-reached themselves and for various reasons construction sometimes took longer than anticipated. One developer found that the builder could not complete the house because he 'goes to the West Indies', though whether to avoid bankruptcy, or to manage his affairs out there, is not said.[32]

The one exception to Tully's terrace plan was the grandest house in the street, Observatory House at its eastern end.[33] It was built at the end of the 1780s for John Davies, tobacconist and snuff maker, and stood full square and detached with an observatory 'on the top floor … covered with heavy lcad'.[34]

Throughout these decades, on the summit of the hill, development also continued eastwards.[35] The western section of what was later

18   *Somerset Street, south–west face.*

known as Kingsdown Parade was in the Upper Montagues, and the remainder was in Kingsdown Mead. The development of the two fields differed: in the Upper Montagues the street was completed on the north side by enlarging existing houses and building in their gardens, and on the south by building further sizeable houses surrounded by gardens. In Kingsdown Mead, however, the houses were built in terraced form, in the eclectic mix of style and size similar to that of Somerset Street.

The 1775 Directory lists 13 residents of Kingsdown Parade and though the 1785 one still has only 13 names, deeds would indicate that this must be an underestimate. As with Somerset Street, it would seem that most of the houses in this section of the Parade were completed by the early 1790s.

In the same period development also started on the fields across Horfield Road, between Southwell Street and Clarence Place—Three Cornered Handkerchief and Green Close. Though soon considered part of Kingsdown, these fields were not former St James Priory land but part of another ecclesiastical establishment to the north, Westbury College in Westbury on Trym.

20 and 21   *A plethora of exuberant bows and canted bays, in stone or wood, some two or even three storeys high. The Somerset Street ones (right) were designed to enjoy that 'view and prospect' across to Lansdown and Dundry; the Back of Kingsdown Parade ones (above centre) looked north over the fields later to be covered by the houses of Cotham.*

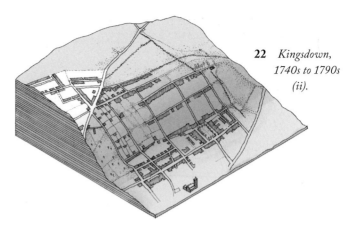

22   *Kingsdown,
1740s to 1790s
(ii).*

There is an advertisement of 1761 for the sale of land and houses which including 'a great house' in Southwell Street, and a decade later in 1773 a minute of the Council records a complaint from some owners of property of Kingsdown and St Michael's Hill 'that they had within a few years built many new houses there, but were discouraged from making further improvements owing to the great damage done to the property by the populace during the execution of criminals and praying that the gallows [sited where St Michael's Hill meets Cotham Road] be removed to Brandon Hill'. On the margin of the Council's 1773 minute book was written 'Nothing done herein'.[36] Nevertheless, despite the residents' 'discouragement', development of Green Close continued in the 1780s with the construction of Paul Street, Oxford Street and Clarence Place, together with Alfred Place, Portland Street and Henrietta Street. The streets would seem to have been named in honour of the then High Steward of Bristol, the 3rd Duke of Portland. The Duke's maternal grandparents were the Earl of Oxford and his wife Henrietta; Clarence is possibly the heir apparent to the throne, later William IV, who was created Duke of Clarence in 1789.

The area was damaged in the war and then largely demolished for the development in the 1980s of High Kingsdown, leaving only remnants of many of these streets. Those houses of Alfred Place that survived, with their canted two- or three-storey bay windows down to street level, present a regular face to the street in contrast to the nearby older houses on Kingsdown Parade. Photographs and maps show that there were similar regular terraces in Clarence Place and Oxford Street and 20th-century writers describe Clarence Place as 'massively dignified'[37] and as 'a ... terrace of considerable value architecturally'.[38] Elsewhere on Green Close, Paul Street was a mixture of houses and shops with lodging above, and much of the remaining area was densely populated with alleys and courts leading off the wider streets, housing tradesmen and those of more modest means.[39]

That disgruntled poet of the 1760s had been very rude about the potential occupants of the King's Down.[40] His verses continue:

Each petty Tradesman here must have his Seat,
And vainly thinks thy Height will make him great:
But little things look less the more they rise;
So Wrens may mount until they look like Flies.
Hail brewer e'er too late, and choose thy Spot
Sell off thy Soot, and build thy Kingsdown Cot.
Come hither Pedlars, quit your dusty Stalls,
Here build your Seats, and rise your Garden Walls,
And when you've built it o'er—call it what you will,
'Twill not be KINGSDOWN then, but PEDLAR'S HILL.

There was perhaps some truth in his sentiments. By the 1780s Kingsdown doubtless had a mix of the aspiring as well as the more established middle classes, and a good sprinkling of 'chief' tradesmen in the smaller houses, particularly on the lower slopes.[41]

It was considered a very pleasant place to live. The 1789 *Gentleman's Magazine* comments, 'The suburb called King's-Down abounds with good houses: and as this part stands pleasantly in an elevated situation, removed in some degree from the smoke and noise of the city, additions are frequently made to the number of its inhabitants.' And Matthew's 1794 Bristol Directory notes:

23 *Alfred Place, east face.*

> King's Square … is on a gentle slope at the bottom of Kingsdown-Hill,
> the ascent to which from this square is very steep yet covered with
> houses up to and beyond the summit. The houses are uniformly built
> of brick ornamented with stone; the whole area surrounded by rails and
> lime trees; the walks neatly gravelled; the square clean, wholesome and
> pleasant and well lighted with lamps.

As early as 1755 Latimer records that King Square's residents included several rich families,[42] and 20 years later nearly a third of the 23 residents listed in the 1775 Directory are described as 'Gent', that is 'of private means'. Latimer also comments, 'Number 18[43] … built by a merchant named Ash, cost £3,000.' 1758 deeds of an apparently similar King Square house state that the developer should build at a cost of 'at least £350'—so it must have had a very luxurious interior finish. The Ash mentioned by Latimer was Edward Ash (d. 1818),[44] who had made his fortune from the manufacture of sweets, raisin wine and raspberry brandy—and from marrying the heiress of the Ashley estate on which Montpelier is built.

Another early resident of King Square was the pastor of the Huguenot Church,[45] the Rev. Pierre Gautier (d. 1791), pastor of the church between 1758-91. During the last quarter of the 17th century over three hundred Huguenot refugees, escaping religious persecution in France, had settled in Bristol and by the middle of the next century, when Gautier fled to Bristol from Normandy and became pastor of their church, most of the Huguenots were firmly established in Bristol trade and society. Some were now third-generation Bristolian and many had inter-married. In consequence the French church was in severe decline, its members drifting into the more fashionable Anglican city churches, or into the new Methodist movement.

Gautier, by all accounts a cheerful, well-liked man, was unable to prevent the downward slide. He also suffered from an ever-decreasing stipend and an extremely difficult senior deacon, Isaac Piguenit. The deacon waged continuous war on his pastor: in 1763, after one particular spat over Gautier's inadvertent omission of the Creed, he had 500 handbills printed condemning the priest, many of which he had stuck on the walls and railings of Gautier's house in King Square, while others he pushed through neighbours' letter-boxes. Poor Madame Gautier was so overcome that the doctor had to be called at midnight. This long-suffering lady helped to supplement the family income from 1762 by running 'A Boarding and Day School for the Instruction of Young Ladies in the French Language and other accomplishments' from their house.

In 1791 Gautier died and with his death the Huguenot religious community virtually ceased to exist as a distinct entity. The wife of one

24 *Views south from Kingsdown Parade of Lansdown (top) and Dundry (bottom), third and fourth drawings from T.L.S. Rowbotham's panorama 'View south from Kingsdown', 1830.*

Mrs. GAUTIER,
Wife of the Rev. Mr. GAUTIER, Minifter to the *French*
CHURCH at BRISTOL,

BEGS Leave to inform the PUBLIC, particu-
larly the Gentry refiding in that City, and neighbouring Country,
that fhe fhall in the Beginning of *April* next, OPEN
A BOARDING and DAY-SCHOOL,
For the Inftruction of Young Ladies in the *French* Language, in its
utmoft Purity and Perfection ; for which Purpofe, fhe has taken a very
convenient Houfe, in a pleafant and healthy Situation, in the New
Square, near Stokes-Croft ; where young Ladies may alfo be inftructed in
every other Branch of polite Education, fuch as fine NEEDLE-WORK,
WRITING, DANCING, MUSICK, &c. proper Affiftants being
engaged for that Purpofe : At the fame Time the greateft Care will be
taken to cultivate their Minds with the Principles of true Religion and
Virtue ; and that the Reading of their own Language may not be neglected, a Portion of Time will be fet apart for that Purpofe ; when
due Regard will be had to the Ladies Reading with proper *Accent*, and
Emphafis.
☞ If this Undertaking fhould meet with Encouragement, there
will be no Pains fpared to render it deferving of the Publick's Favour.

25 *Mme Gautier's school, King Square (*Felix Farley's Bristol Journal, *20 March 1762).*

of his successors wrote that the congregation was now composed almost entirely of English people 'fond of French or those wishing to improve'.

Although the Protestant Huguenot religion was tolerated, there was little sufferance for Roman Catholicism in 18th-century Kingsdown, or in Bristol as a whole. Indeed the Catholic priest historian George Oliver wrote in 1857, 'From the so-called Reformation until the accession of George II, in no commercial city of the British Empire was Catholic faith and practice more discouraged and depressed than in Bristol.'[46] In St James's parish in 1766-7 only 53 people admitted to being 'Papists'[47] and, around this time, when a Mr Coppinger, a well-qualified teacher, attempted to open a school in Kingsdown, 'at first his prospects were favourable, but when it was discovered that he was Papist, every hope of success vanished and he was compelled to decamp'.[48]

In contrast the Methodist movement was in the ascendancy in the city and its founder, John Wesley (1703-91), often preached in the open air to large crowds, a regular venue in Bristol being Carolina Court, immediately behind King Square, or sometimes the Square itself. In the diary John Wesley kept of his journeying—he travelled some 5,000 miles a year for over 50 years and preached over 40,000 sermons—he writes of his initial misgivings about open-air preaching:

> 1739 … in the evening I reached Bristol and met Mr. Whitefield there I could scarce reconcile myself at first to this strange habit of preaching in the fields, of which he set me an example on Sunday: having been all my life (till very lately) so tenacious of every point relating to decency and order, that I should have thought the saving of souls almost a sin, if it had not been done in a church.

However, nearly 40 years and many open-air sermons later, he records, '1781 … in the calm, sun shiny evening I preached near King's Square: I know nothing more solemn than such a congregation praising God with one heart and one voice. Surely they who talk of the indecency of field-preaching never saw such a sight as this.'

The King Square site is regularly mentioned in the *Journals*, often with comment on the size of the congregation there. The very last time was when Wesley was 87, at the end of August 1790. It was one of his last sermons in the open air; he was old and by his own account his strength had quite forsaken him, though he continued to travel and preach nevertheless. He died just six months later in March 1791.[49]

26   *John Wesley preaching in the open air off King Square. Illustration from* Wesley: his own biographer, Selections from the Journals, *1891.*

For the last twenty years of his life Wesley had been one of the main activists in the fight to abolish the slave trade. Many of the sermons he gave in or near King Square would have contained the case for the liberty and humanitarian treatment of slaves and he must have been very aware of the profits of that trade in the nearby houses and on the slopes above.

One such contemporary house owner in Kingsdown Parade, whose wealth came both directly and indirectly from slavery, was Robert Lucas (1705-74),[50] living in one of the large houses at the west end of the street.[51] Described in deeds as a 'hooper'—one involved with the manufacture and fastening of hoops on casks, barrels and ships—he would have benefited indirectly from the fitting out of slave ships for the African coast. He also benefited directly as a shareholder in at least three slaving voyages, in 1756, 1757 and 1774. The first, that of the *Prince Edward*, ended in early disaster when it was taken by a French privateer 45 leagues west of Lundy and escorted into a French port.[52] Undeterred, some ten months later he is registered as one of three part-owners of the *Mercury*, which is recorded as selling 354 slaves at St Kitts and returning safely.[53]

A close neighbour and friend of Lucas also involved in slavery was the ship's captain, John Chilcott (d. 1780). Chilcott, who had bought Marlborough House on Jane Jones's death in 1751, was a leading agent of Bristol slaving voyages. Early in his career he was master of slave ships from Bristol and later, as he made his money, part shareowner of two dozen or so such voyages. Not that voyages were always profitable, as Lucas had discovered a decade earlier. In 1776 the *Africa,* of which Chilcott was part shareowner, *en route* to West Africa to buy gold, ivory, rice and slaves, was blown up off Portugal in an engagement with an American privateer.[54] In 1779, as slaving became less profitable and the abolitionists were in the ascendant, he moved to privateering himself, advertising for sailors to fight against Spain in his frigate *Mars*, 'the most complete private ship of war in Great Britain'. It was perhaps not the safest of career moves, though, for the following year John Chilcott was dead and the house occupied by his widow.

As Chilcott had found, by the last decades of the century 'the ardour for the trade to Africa for men and women, our fellow creatures and equals, was much abated among the humane and benevolent Merchants of Bristol'.[55] However, while deploring the continuation of the trade in Liverpool the merchants of Bristol were quite content to continue to profit from the work of the slaves in the overseas plantations—in particular the production of sugar and hardwoods. The sweets, raisin wine and raspberry brandy of Edward Ash, resident in King Square, would all have used sugar from the plantations in Jamaica; and Georgian houses were lavish users of mahogany in both their fixtures and their fittings, the wood being cut in the rainforests of Central America by slaves imported from Africa.

A major developer of Georgian Bristol and consequent user of much of that mahogany was James Lockier (1740-1802), director of the timber merchants Lockier Macaulay & Co. Lockier was Robert Lucas's son-in-law, and was himself resident in Kingsdown Parade from 1770-4. It would seem that in the main he invested any profits he made in property development, but at least once he followed Lucas's example and was part shareholder in 1791/2 in a ship doing the triangular route. *The Lioness*, which travelled from Bristol via Africa to Honduras, is recorded returning to Bristol laden with mahogany and other wood.[56]

James Lockier was to be the developer behind many of the more spectacular Bristol terraces, including Berkeley Crescent (1787), Portland Square (1790), and Royal York Crescent (1790). More domestically, in the 1780s he was also at work on a smaller scale at the west end of Kingsdown Parade. Following his widowed mother-in-law's death he had bought the Lucas house, together with the garden next door, from his wife's brother.

FOR SALE (in Fee) by AUCTION,
— At the EXCHANGE COFFEE-HOUSE, in the
ity of Briſtol, by order of the Aſſignees of JAMES
OCKIER, a Bankrupt, on THURSDAY the 13th day
f February, 1794, at one o'clock in the Afternoon
reciſely,

All that capital Meſſuage or Tene-
ment, lately occupied by the ſaid James Lockier, ſitu-
e on Kingſdown, in the pariſh of St. James, in the
ounty of Gloceſter, with the Garden thereunto belong-
g, and in which there is a capital Hot-houſe or forcing
ouſe not long ſince erected in a very maſterly ſtile, and
t a very conſiderable expence.——The whole of the
round, including that upon which the Houſe ſtands,
ontains in breadth in the front towards Kingſdown,
o feet or nearly thereabout, and in depth backwards
f the ſame breadth or nearly ſo throughout, 130 feet.

The Houſe comprizes on the ground-floor a very good
itchen 18 feet by 17 feet, with grate, ſmoke jack,
ven, &c. compleat, a back kitchen with large furnace
nd boiler, ſpring and rain water pumps, kitchen pan-
y, two cellars, and a laundry 23 feet by 12.—— Fire
arlour floor—a drawing room 23 feet 6 inches by 18
et; a dining parlour 18 by 17; breakfaſt parlour 18
y 12 feet 6 inches; ſtudy 13 by 11; and a china cloſet.
The Firſt Chamber ſtory,—four bed rooms ſame di-
enſions as the rooms below it, with water cloſet and
rge ciſtern above.
The Attick ſtory, comprizes 4 bed rooms, with clo-
ts to each, and a dreſſing room,
Over which there are very ſpacious garrets.
The Garden is handſomely laid out, and the Hot-
ouſe is 45 feet long by 15 feet deep.
The whole is ſubject to a fee-farm rent of £8 only.

☞ For a view of the Premiſes, further particulars,
nd conditions of ſale, apply to William Gibbons. Eſq.
Mr. Benjamin Baugh. and Mr. Philip Jones, Aſſignees
o the Bankrupt's eſtate; or to Mr. James Weekes or
Mr. Iſaac Cooke, their ſolicitors; or to Mr. James
ughes, Attorney at Law, Corn-ſtreet, Briſtol:
                    JOS. BONBONOUS, Broker.

27   *Advertisement,* Felix Farley's Bristol Journal, *25 January 1794. An unusually full sales advertisement for no. 10 Kingsdown Parade completed and sold by Lockier's bankruptcy trustees. It gives some idea of the living arrangements of a well-appointed Georgian Kingsdown household—with the addition of such sophistications as a smokejack, a water closet and a conservatory.*

In Georgian times cooking was still done on an open grate with spit over and oven usually alongside. In more sophisticated houses, as here, the simple jack for turning the spit had been replaced by one using gears turned by the hot air rising from the grate.

Water closets (here one is sited on the first floor) were beginning to come in during the second half of the century among the better off, but would have been by no means common in Kingsdown. It would have been mechanically washed with water from the cistern above, the cistern filled daily by a servant pumping water up.

The hothouse in the garden, shown on the 1885 OS map to have run alongside the Parade wall, would certainly have been quite unusual in the 18th century. The OS shows glasshouses in many of the Kingsdown gardens, but most of these would have been Victorian additions. Not until the early 19th century did improvements in technology lead to cheaper glass and cast iron, putting conservatories within the reach of most middle-class citizens. The garden itself would have been formally laid out with straight gravel avenues flanked by narrow beds and well-ordered trees. The grass lawns and more fluid lines on the OS map are Victorian.

He improved and enlarged the family house on the north-westward part of the plot, doubling it in size; and then on the adjacent garden site he began to build an equally imposing establishment.[57] The extended house he rented out on completion, but next door was possibly intended for his own residence if the advertisement is to be believed.

Formal Kingsdown, 1790s

By the final decades of the century, Bristol's status in the country, both as a port and a city, was beginning to decline, although it continued to be a major trading centre for the south-west. Bristol merchants continued to deal successfully and profitably across the Atlantic but, with the movement to abolish the slave trade gathering strength, many had withdrawn from the African trade. The Industrial Revolution was, however, centred on the north and the Midlands and the passageway up the Avon was increasingly hazardous for ever larger ships. Moreover, Bristol's merchants, the critics said, were less aggressively competitive than those of her rivals, Liverpool, Manchester and Birmingham.

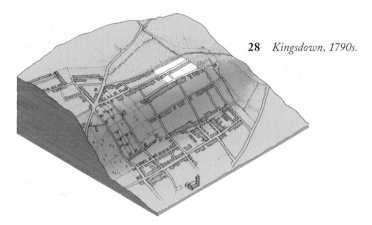

28   *Kingsdown, 1790s.*

Despite such warning signs, Bristol's housing boom initially continued apace. During these years, the main development of Clifton commenced spectacularly with the grand terraces of Cornwallis and Royal York Crescent, Richmond and Windsor Terraces, and the Paragon all starting between 1789 and 1792. At the same time the last piece of the jigsaw of the development of the former Priory fields on the King's Down was laid in place. In 1791 James Lockier, having purchased with others the remainder of Kingsdown field in 1785, began developing the eastern half of Kingsdown Parade, then known as St James Place.[58]

Georgian architecture had become more sophisticated since the earlier decades of the century. Unlike the remainder of Kingsdown Parade, these houses were planned as two uniform and formal terraces, possibly to the design of the Paty office. There were to be 21 five-storey houses on the south and 19 four-storey houses on the north side of the street. And, significantly, Lockier laid down in the agreements detailed specifications for the design and construction of the houses. Although the actual work on the buildings was, as previously, contracted out to smaller builders, now every detail of the exterior dimensions and materials to be used was specified.

31   *The 1785 plans for St James Place at the eastern end of Kingsdown Parade.*

NORTHSIDE   E

The north side of St James Place was designed unusually as linked pairs of houses, except for the middle three, which were designed as a formal central threesome. The hallway was separated out as a two-storey wing, providing a solution that was aesthetically pleasing and gave the occupier the perceived benefits of being semi-detached. The south side was a terrace of more conventional paired houses of uniform height.

The original plan for the north side was not to be. Already by the end of 1792 it was becoming obvious that those involved had overstretched themselves. During that year James Lockier and his fellow developer made various loans to builders in an attempt to get the houses on St James Place completed, Lockier borrowing large sums himself to do so, and in December the Merchant Venturers, concerned about his ability to complete Royal York Crescent, floated a loan subscription to try and rescue that terrace.

Two months later, in February 1793, the French declared war. There was financial panic throughout the country and Bristol, its financial base already crumbling with over-speculation in housing development, was hit by severe recession. Builders and developers alike went bankrupt and all building stopped. In Bristol and its suburbs, it is said, more than 500 houses in course of construction were left unfinished, and the appearance of the suburbs reminded strangers of a place that had undergone bombardment.[59]

29 *(Top left) Kingsdown Parade. St James's Place, north side; in the middle Lockier's original grand design, on the right the 'gaps' infilled.*

30 *(Top right) Kingsdown Parade. St James's Place, south side— the façades little changed from Lockier's original design.*

SOUTHSIDE ELEVATION

James Lockier and his firm Lockier Macaulay were declared bankrupt in May 1793. His late father-in-law's house at the west end of Kingsdown Parade was sold at auction in August 1793 and the house next door was completed by his executors and similarly sold in January of the following year. In September 1793 all the 'unfinished hereditaments and premises' of St James Place were sold at auction at the *Full Moon* tavern in Stokes Croft.

The two terraces were bought by his fellow developer James Weekes and his son Robert, and over the coming decades that family slowly continued the development. The Weekes had, however, been owed a lot of money by Lockier and shared none of his vision for the 'uniformity of the said range'. In the delay the north side of St James Place was to lose much of its original form, for the two of them, preferring to maximise their profit, placed no restrictions on the various builders of the north side. In consequence the later houses of that terrace sacrificed the uniformity and elegance of the original design to gain extra accommodation by infilling over the entrance wings. Today James Lockier's grand vision can still be easily seen in only two of the paired houses.[60]

On the south side, where the original design of the terrace remains largely unchanged, the Weekes sold off separately the lower part of most of the houses' long gardens. At either end of this 'strip', stretching along Somerset Street between Spring Hill and Thomas Street, plots were sold and soon built on—as Spring Hill Villa and Somerset Cottage— but the remainder of the land was purchased by the Weekes' fellow developer Robert Gay for use as front 'display' gardens for the Somerset Street houses opposite that he and his daughter lived in. In the late 1780s he had built three grand houses at the eastern end of Somerset Street—selling one, giving one in marriage settlement to his daughter, but keeping the third for his own occupation.[61]

Though each successive year saw more occupants of St James Place, the development was not finished for another twenty years. The first three houses were occupied in 1795 and the north side was completed in 1802. The south side was not ready until 1815.

The only other notable building in Kingsdown during the last decade of the century was Portland Chapel. The popularity of the Methodist movement in Bristol had continued to gather momentum over the 18th century, with John Wesley's New Room, the original chapel in Broadmead below, becoming increasingly crowded. Finally, in the 1790s the Methodists decided that the time had come for the growing population of Kingsdown to have its own chapel, and so Portland Chapel, 'The Chapel on the Hill', opened in Portland Street in 1792.[62]

32   *Nos 23-5 Somerset Street, the three houses built by Robert Gay at the western end of the street with their front 'display' gardens across the road.*

One of the main movers in the chapel's foundation was Capt. Thomas Webb (d. 1796), himself resident in Portland Street.[63] Webb was a flamboyant figure in the Methodist movement. A member of the British army until 1764 and in action in Canada under General Wolfe, he converted to Methodism during a visit to England in 1765. On his return to America he became very active in Methodist affairs, and was a founder member of the first Methodist chapel in America in New York in 1768. A charismatic preacher, dressed in regimental scarlet, a black patch over his right eye (lost in action), and his sword lying across the Bible on the desk beside him, he delivered his sermons in eloquent and fiery style. In 1778, however, he was accused of spying for the British government in the American War of Independence and sent back to England—settling eventually in Kingsdown in 1792.

By the 1790s the Methodist movement was over 50 years old, and following John Wesley's death in 1791 some of the restrictions he had insisted on, in particular that communion could be received only from ordained Anglican clergy, were being challenged as out of date by some members, the self-styled 'New Planners'. The newly founded chapel in Kingsdown preached a more radical message than its parent and conflict was inevitable. In 1794 one of its trustees, banned from preaching at the New Room because of his previous celebration of communion at Portland Chapel, quietly read the Attorney's letter, then folding it leisurely said: 'Though the Trustees have the power to prevent me preaching on their premises, yet they cannot restrain me from proclaiming the grace of God. I shall therefore proceed up the hill to the Portland Chapel where the Gospel is not bound.' As one the congregation cried, 'We will all follow you,' and attended by a great concourse of people they came up the heights to Portland.[64]

In all some 800 members left the New Room over the controversy, causing its closure and the building of a replacement chapel in the centre of the city which followed a less traditional line.

The Regency Decades, 1800-30s

The end of the Napoleonic War in 1815 saw an improvement in the economy of what was still a prosperous trading city. Nevertheless, with only a limited amount of industrialisation in its immediate hinterland,

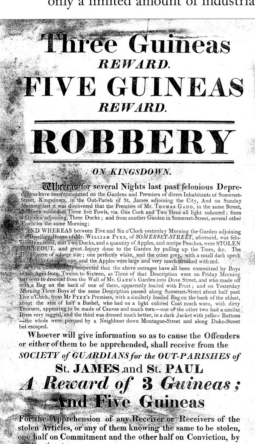

33 *Petty crime was rife in Georgian and Victorian England and Millerd, in his maps from 1673 to 1728, had written on St Michael's Hill, 'not far from here the way narrows, beware of thieves and prostitutes'. Kingsdown, however, was until 1835 mainly without the boundaries of Bristol, in the county of Gloucestershire, and as such was considered to be outside of the city's jurisdiction. Consequently, as recorded in Latimer's 18th-century* Annals of Bristol, *the residents decided in 1783 to hire vigilantes themselves, advertising for 'a few able-bodied young men to be employed as a nightly patrol' in the locality which came to be known as 'The Society of Guardians for the Out-Parishes of St James'.*

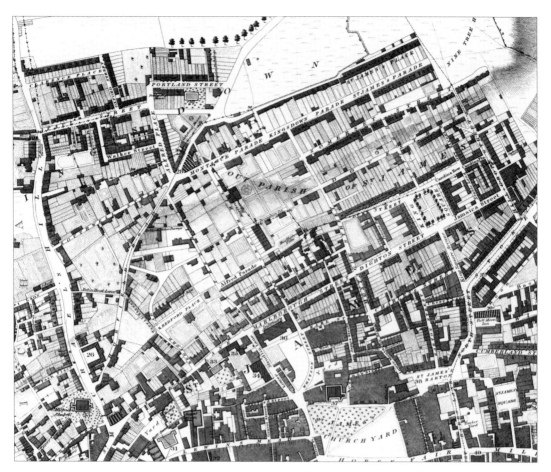

34 *Detail from Ashmead's Map of Bristol 1828. Most of Kingsdown as we now know it is covered with buildings, but Cotham is still just fields. The contrast between the early Georgian suburban-style development of the Upper Montagues and the later Georgian style of Dove Croft, Prior's Hill and Kingsdown Mead is clearly seen.*

Bristol became only the eighth rather than the second most important port in terms of vessels and tonnage, and although in 1809 works to the Floating Harbour had been successfully completed to provide more predictable berthing, the long and hazardous passage up the Avon remained a limitation.

Building activity throughout the city and its suburbs had been hard hit by the recession of the turn of the century, with many resultant bankruptcies of developers, investors and builders, and when development started again it was at first very subdued. In Kingsdown the early decades of the new century saw the finishing of the many houses left half built, with the only new house building of note being a small terrace, Marlborough Hill Place off Marlborough Hill, completed around 1831, and Devon House, the most imposing house in Kingsdown Parade, built in the side garden of its neighbour *c.*1818.[65]

35   *Marlborough Hill Place.*

The land to the north-east of Kingsdown, where Cotham now starts, was to remain all but unbuilt on for another forty years. There had been plans in the 1790s to continue development northwards, on the field immediately to the north-east of Kingsdown Parade. Foundations were laid for a crescent of houses and a brick-kiln was erected by the builders, but when recession hit, the scheme had been abandoned and the brick-kiln was converted into a cow-house.[66]

The only construction to be realised on this field in the period was St Matthew's Church, consecrated in 1835. Throughout the 18th century, as the suburb of Kingsdown grew, the two parish churches in the area, St James's and St Michael's, had been complaining of their difficulties in accommodating ever increasing congregations. In 1775 the main body of St Michael's was demolished and a new church built, and in 1785 the parish of St James was subdivided and the new parish of St Paul's formed, its parish church in Portland Square being completed in 1794. It was to be another forty years before the decision was taken to build a new church on the summit of the hill, when in 1833 the evangelical vicar of St James's, the Rev. Thomas Biddulph, a resident of Kingsdown Parade, took the initiative.

36   *St Matthew's Church, 1835.*

Biddulph gathered together a group of local worthies who between themselves—unusually, because most churches at this time were dependent on diocesan aid—raised the necessary capital by private subscription. As trustees, they negotiated to buy the land and commissioned the architect Thomas Rickman, regarded as an expert in Gothic Revivalism. In April 1835 the Anglicans of Kingsdown at last had their own separate church—and a survey done in 1881 on Bristol churchgoers recorded 621 worshippers there in the morning and 466 in the evening.

During the decades of the 1800s-30s there was widespread disaffection with government, both national and local, and with authority in general. The unrest was mainly in support of national political reform, but was also an expression of growing discontent among the lower classes at their depressed living standards. In 1831 Bristol erupted in riot. Crowds looted and destroyed many of the buildings in Queen Square and around, broke into the main gaol, and generally controlled the city for the best part of three days.

Following the riot, the city authorities tried to stop any future civic disorder by increasing policing and enforcing crowd control legislation. In particular, crowds celebrating 5 November were banned within the city centre. Each year feelings ran high in Bristol on that day. The anniversary of the foiling of the Guy Fawkes plot was regarded by the anti-papists as an opportunity to display their anti-Catholic feelings, by the politically aware as a continuing expression of their disaffection, and by others as an excuse for riotous behaviour. On being banned from the city centre, the crowds merely dispersed to the nearest part of Bristol outside the city boundary—Kingsdown.

As the *Bristol Mirror* reported in 1838:

> We regret that in the evening of this day [5 November] a serious disturbance took place in the neighbourhood of the *Montague Tavern*, in consequence of the efforts made by the police to carry into effect the orders of the magistrates, prohibiting the discharge of fireworks in the public streets. For some years past a considerable assembly of young men and boys have much annoyed the neighbourhood of Kingsdown by their riotous conduct on this anniversary, which may be partly accounted for by its having been the line of separation between the ancient city and the adjoining county, and therefore a species of debatable ground or no-man's land.[67]

The defence offered—that the offence for which the lads were charged was committed outside of the city—had been dismissed by the magistrates some years earlier,[68] and in any case after 1835 the boundary changes made this no longer an accurate excuse. The seasonal disturbances, however—in which crackers, squibs and stones were thrown, windows smashed and gas lamps shattered, and policemen, rioters and innocent Kingsdown residents injured and frightened—went on for many years. A very full report of the disorder five years after the riots states that:

> It appears that on the night of the 5th November a number of young men armed with bludgeons assembled together on Kingsdown; they appeared to act in concert, and at the cry of 'Union', a kind of watchword, they commenced destroying the gas lamps, breaking in the windows of the different houses with their sticks, and actually carrying their insane mirth so far as to fire a heavily loaded pistol through the door of Mr. Keyser's house.[69]

The residents of Kingsdown were understandably much bothered by the violent and excited crowd and the damage being done to their houses. A Mr Pym of Kingsdown Parade gave evidence that 'on hearing my window broken, I ran into the street … and much frightened I went in and bolted my door'.[70] Poor Miss English further down the Parade[71] found herself the unwilling observer of the riotous behaviour. In her evidence she states that, hearing 'a noise of persons huzzaing at the Back of Kingsdown', she went out thinking that some fireworks were going to be displayed, saw a large party breaking the gas lamp to pieces, and 'her sister, who was alarmed, drew another person, in mistake into the house, and fastened her out'!

There are reports of arrests in the papers throughout these decades.[72] A cross-section of society was apparently involved in the disturbances, the *Bristol Mirror* reporting that offenders ranged from one 'who described himself as an Oxford Student' and was fined 10s., to 'a little urchin of the sooty tribe' who was given a good character reference and let off with a caution.[73]

Some thirty years later, though, as society's problems eased in Bristol, the *Bristol Times* lamented that bonfire night had become 'decidedly dull'.[74]

All these disturbances 'took place in the neighbourhood of the *Montague Tavern*', and undoubtedly drink also played a part in the rioting, for the inn was a popular drinking place where alcohol flowed liberally. A bill of 1817 showed a dozen dinner guests averaging three bottles of wine apiece;[75] and an inventory of 1850 lists its cellars as containing 424 bottles of vintage port, 142 bottles of ordinary port and

37   *The* Montague Inn *at the west end of Kingsdown Parade, 1938.*

61 bottles of champagne and spirits, along with claret, sauterne, sherry, sparkling marsala, pineapple rum and punch.[76]

As the Kingsdown fields were built over, the *Montague* became increasingly well known, favoured both by residents and those from further afield. It was particularly famous for its turtle soup and other turtle delicacies, the creatures transported alive to Bristol from the West Indies in large tanks.

In the 19th century, as an article in the *Western Daily Press* in the 1940s recalled, 'the *Montague* was easily the most popular rendezvous in the city for annual and other festive occasions'. The article told how for many years the local survivors of the Battle of Waterloo and later those of the First World War held their annual dinner there; how the Bristol Madrigal Society, founded in 1837, held its inaugural and many subsequent meetings there; and how it was the recognised meeting place

38   *The Music Room at the* Montague Hotel, *with the tables arranged for a meeting of the Bristol Madrigal Society. The Bristol Madrigal Society, now the Bristol Chamber Choir, held its initial meeting at the* Montague *in 1837 and continued to meet there until the 20th century. One of its founders was Robert Lucas Pearsall (1795-1856), the well-known amateur composer, and it was primarily for this society that Pearsall wrote his many madrigals, part-songs and sacred music. More parochially, Pearsall was the great-great-grandson of Henry Dighton, the 17th-century owner of the Kingsdown fields, and spent his boyhood, from 1811-17, in no. 6 Somerset Street.*

39   *Advertisement for turtle soup at the Montague Tavern, 1796.*

for the local Tories and 'leading philanthropic and benevolent organisations'. It continued to be famous for its turtle soup and other delicacies: an article in the 1837 *Bristol Mirror* reported that 'Mine host of the *Montague Hotel* … has been honoured with an order for 40 quarts of his famous turtle soup by the Duke of Wellington. It is for the anniversary dinner of the Battle of Waterloo his grace gives every year.' And nearly fifty years later, in 1883, the members of the Thorne Club, old boys and sixth formers of Bristol Grammar School, who dined there commented that it 'well maintained on this occasion its deserved reputation'.

At the *Montague*'s peak it even spilled over into the garden of the cottage opposite, across the Parade. There could be found a cottage or 'summer house'[77] with a Turtle Room (presumably with turtles swimming in a tank), a Card Room, a Billiard Room, a Bowling Alley and a garden. The 1850 inventory states that the inn had a total of 27 rooms, of which only nine were bedrooms.

As Kingsdown's fortunes declined during the early 20th century, the *Montague*, too, became less fashionable, more shabby and run-down. When in 1942 a part of the building was badly damaged in an air raid, the owners decided to pull down the rest. Today there is no visible trace of the inn;[78] its site and that of its immediate neighbours are grassed over and the only reminder is that the open space created is called Montague Green.[79]

THREE

From Suburb to Inner City

In the early decades of the Victorian era Bristol entered a new, more settled, age. Its economy continued to grow throughout the century, albeit at a more sedate rate than its northern rivals. Despite the limitations of its inland port, tonnage of trade continued to increase and in 1841 Brunel's Great Western Railway, connecting Bristol with London, reached the city. Firms producing consumer goods such as tobacco, chocolate and wine provided an ever-increasing share of the commercial wealth of the city. In the 1870s, after much wrangling, Avonmouth and Portishead docks were opened downriver and Brunel's broad gauge railway was converted to the width used elsewhere, allowing easier access to and from the rest of the country.

As a direct consequence Bristol's population grew from 69,000 at the beginning of the 19th century to nearly 324,000 by the end, with people flocking from the countryside for work. The Victorian suburbs of Bristol, aided from 1875 by the development of the tram, sprawled far beyond its original boundaries, and Kingsdown became a part of the inner city.

Early and Mid-Victorian Decades

The development of Cotham, to the north of Kingsdown, started in the 1840s. Nine Tree Field and Pugsley's Well Field, the two fields between the north-eastern side of Kingsdown and Cotham Road, had also once been Priory fields. They were sold in the 17th century by the Somerset family to a Bristol merchant, John Edwards, and by the 19th century they had passed to Edwards' great-grandson, the Right Hon. Thomas Fremantle. The two closes of meadow, or pasture ground, were named at that point as 'formerly three closes, heretofore called by the several names of Harpe Close, Whorestone and the Upper Barnsdall, but now called Steep Hill and Conduit Close',[1] though later deeds call the two fields Nine Tree Field (after the nine elms that stood on the site of Fremantle Square until the early 19th century) and Pugsley's Well Field.

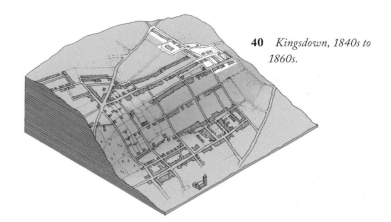

40   *Kingsdown, 1840s to 1860s.*

To the north west, the adjoining Kendal Mead was not ex-Priory land, but originally part of the land belonging to Westbury College. By the 18th century it had become a part of the estate of Redland Court, but during the 19th century the estate was sold to settle debts, subsequently passing through the hands of various property speculators. Development of this field—where St Matthews Road and Cotham Road South are now—did not begin until the 1860s.

On the fields owned by Fremantle, Nine Tree Field and Pugsley's Well Field, most of the land was covered in houses during the 1840s and '50s. Sir Thomas Fremantle had married the daughter of Sir George Nugent, son of Robert Earl and Viscount Clare, and Queen Victoria had just ascended the throne. The origin of many of the names in the area are thus explained: Fremantle Square and Road, Nugent Hill, Clare Road, Victoria Walk and Gardens and, below the summit, Thomas Street and Nine Tree Hill.

There was no reminder in the naming of the earlier battles fought on the site, but during this time a number of Civil War finds were made around the site of Prior's Hill fort.[2] When the ground was being excavated in 1835, workmen found near the front garden of no. 1 Fremantle Square a considerable number of lead bullets, tobacco pipes and small measures that would hold a charge of powder for the muskets.[3] Seven skeletons were also discovered in the area and were buried, by the direction of the coroner, in the green of the Square.[4] By the early 19th century the substantial mound on which Prior's Hill Fort had stood had been destroyed by levelling and erosion.[5]

The period from the late 1830s to the 1850s represents a watershed in popular demand and architectural style, both in Bristol and throughout England, and the change is neatly exemplified in these streets. Three sides of Fremantle Square and most of the houses on the western side of Fremantle Road (*c*.1840) continued the terrace pattern, albeit in a

41 *Fremantle Square, north-east side.*

42 *Fremantle Square, north-west side.*

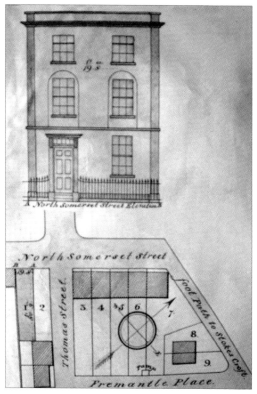

43 *Elevation from 1836 deeds of no. 1 North Somerset Street. Nos 1 and 2 were subsequently renumbered as nos 41 and 42 in Somerset Street. Nos 4-7 became part of Fremantle Square.*

pleasing adaptation by the architect William Armstrong of the classical Regency style. In contrast, the fourth side of the square (1850s) and the east side of the road (1850s-70s) were designed as the newly fashionable semi-detached suburban villas that were every middle-class Victorian's ideal home.

At the eastern ends of Somerset Street and Kingsdown Parade the final houses also reflect this change in architectural style. The terraced houses at the east end of Somerset Street,[6] built in the late 1830s and early 1840s, are identical to the houses on the south and west sides of Fremantle Square. In contrast Apsley Villas, built in 1840 at the end of Kingsdown Parade, is a pair of imposing semi-detached villas.

Victorian lawyers had become less verbose than Georgian ones, though house deeds were still more prescriptive than today. Where Georgian deeds had even banned specific antisocial activities on the part of the residents,[7] those for Fremantle Square now stated, more relevantly, that the builder developer 'should immediately after said house was covered in, insure and keep insured in some proper Insurance

Office against fire'. Until 1877 Bristol had no comprehensive city fire brigade and houses were dependent on either the parish fireman with his 'two buckets, a pickhook and an axe' or, as here, insuring themselves. The insurance offices owned their own fire engines but would only attend their clients' fires so insured houses would sport fire marks on their façades indicating which company they were with. Such marks can still be seen on the front of several Kingsdown houses: on one in Kingsdown Parade for example is the Crown Insurance Fire Office mark and in Montague Hill one of the Sun Fire Office.

Prior to the development of the Fremantle lands, Pugsley's Well field (to the north-east of Kingsdown) had been a favoured place for the citizens of Bristol to take the air now that the fields of the King's Down were built on. In particular they would visit the well or spring, known in the early 18th century as the Virgin's Well but, by the late 18th century and 19th century, as Pugsley's, or Mother Pugsley's, or Dame Pugsley's Well.

The romantic story of Dame Pugsley has been cherished—and probably embroidered—over the years. It tells how among those slain in the Civil War battle of 1645 was a recently married young Royalist officer, Captain Pugsley. On the orders of General Fairfax, the officer was buried with military honours in the field where he fell, adjoining the fort.[8] His young widow, who never remarried, survived him for some sixty years, devoting herself to charitable works and spending much of her time beside the well, ministering to the sick who came there in search of a cure for sore and inflamed eyes. She was reputed to be especially fond of children, and they of her, encouraging them to play in the field beside what came to be called Mother Pugsley's Well.

On her death it is said that she was buried in accordance with her dying wish by her husband's side, wearing her wedding dress and wound in her wedding sheet. She was borne to her grave on an open bier, accompanied by young girls strewing flowers and herbs, and with a musician playing merrily, and the funeral was watched by at least ten thousand spectators.

Documented facts about the couple are notably lacking. The story was not mentioned by Barrett in his *History of Bristol*, published in 1789, and Seyer, the city's most scholarly historian, who wrote a detailed account of the 1645 siege, does not refer to the incident. The first printed account of it appeared in 1824 when John Evans, a resident of Kingsdown Parade, produced his *History of Bristol*.[9] He claimed as his source a contemporary manuscript belonging to a Quaker family named Farnham, but their papers have not survived.

44 *'View of Bristol from Mother Pugsley's Well' by Lt Col. William Booth, 1819. In the background is Observatory House, demolished* c.*1885 to build nos 38-42 Somerset Street, and beyond is St Paul's church in Portland Square.*

Latimer in 1900 records the story, but does not quote his source. St James's parish rate books of 1708, though, do contain an entry that shows a Mother Pugsley being rated for property in the parish in the early 18th century.[10]

The evidence for the existence of a well and springs, later associated with Dame Pugsley, is firmer. It is thought possible that it is the 'Waldes well', referred to as a boundary marker in a document commissioned by King Alfred in 883 to define a part of the boundary of the diocese of Worcester when he was supervising the restoration of church lands appropriated by the laity.[11] Later the priors of St James, it would seem, tapped the spring serving the well, for deeds of 1579 refer to a close of arable land called Upper Barnsdall, 'wherein there is a conduit'.[12] By the early 18th century the name of this piece of land had been changed to Conduit Close, but late 18th-century deeds refer to Pugsley's Well field. By the early 19th century Pugsley's Well was marked on maps and depicted by Bristol artists.

45   *'Mother Pugsley's Well looking towards Somerset Street' by Samuel Jackson, 1823. Observatory House, Somerset Street, is in the background.*

Access in the 19th century was by means of stone steps down to an underground pavement and two basins. An octogenarian, writing to a newspaper in 1910, describes its one-time appearance:

> the so-called well was never a well, but two springs that flowed gently into two basins that were hewn out of a large, long stone. The water from the basin on the left hand was used for curing sore eyes; people would go to the basin early in the morning for this purpose. The other was used for drinking purposes.

He adds:

> the field was used more as a park than anything else; I never saw any cattle in it. Parents used to take their children to fly their kites there. It was the fashion in those days to have the kites about six feet high, and they looked very fine flying over the city when the wind was right,

and Booth's picture of 1819, though without kites, confirms this happy scene.

In 1839 the land was sold for development to the builder John Hucker, a major developer of the Fremantle land over a long period. Bristolians were outraged and appealed to the city to at least preserve the public right of access to the well, but the city decided it could not be justified in such an action. Hucker not only covered the field with houses, but also built a house for himself just below the well (which he named Spring Villa), removed the basins, and diverted the spring to flow into the reservoir of a new well he had dug some yards away on the boundary of his garden.[13]

As time passed and Hucker's further development altered the topography of the slopes, the location of the spring became confused in people's minds, until in 1940 Spring Villa was destroyed in the Blitz. Water Board engineers on the site found beneath the garden boundary wall of the house built in the yard of Hucker's house the 20ft reservoir Hucker had dug.[14] Today a wellhead above a 20ft deep stone-built shaft with about three to four feet of clear water at the bottom can still be seen, though its appearance gives little hint of its feeder spring's legendary past.

Despite the growing popularity of Cotham and beyond in the 1840s and '50s, it was not until a generation later, in the mid-1860s, that Kingsdown began to show signs of change in its social make-up. Examination of census data and deeds before that date show its residents continued to be a mixture of professional and middle classes, commerce and trade, and the large houses generally still in single family occupation. Of the 41 residents of Somerset Street at the time of the 1841 census, a quarter describe themselves as of independent means and another quarter as professionals, with the remainder in commerce or trade, and a similar pattern can be seen in the other streets and in the following two censuses of 1851 and 1861.

Two prosperous Somerset Street residents in commerce during these years were H.O. Wills II, the tobacco magnate, and later his heir H.O. Wills III.[15] By the 1860s their company W.D. & H.O. Wills was one of the largest tobacco manufacturers in Bristol, with 93 employees.

The Wills firm was known for its family spirit and looking after its workers. It pioneered canteens, free medical care, sports facilities and paid holidays—and in 1851 employees were even taken by train to the Great Exhibition at London, each with a sovereign in his pocket. The Wills family were active Congregationalists, and successive generations, true to their nonconformist background, continued to live unostentatiously, giving substantial sums to a variety of good causes, many associated with Bristol. Wills II was a prime mover in the building of Highbury Chapel (now Cotham parish church) and other Congregational churches in the city. His son, Wills III, was a major benefactor to Bristol University, contributing significantly towards its establishment as a fully independent institution.

Today, as Imperial Tobacco, the company is the world's fourth largest tobacco company, with around 14,500 employees worldwide. However, it no longer has a Bristol manufacturing connection: the last Imperial Tobacco cigar was rolled in Bedminster in 2008.

In these times the area would have been much more densely populated than it is today. Victorian middle-class families were often very large: Wills II, who married twice, had 18 children in total and his son 12. Kingsdown census returns show that such a large number of children was not exceptional among local families, while those with six to eight children were commonplace. Moreover, households were often further increased by resident or visiting aunts, nieces, nephews, sisters and grandmothers, and though sons usually left home when they came of age, daughters were commonly expected to stay in the parental home until they married.

Also, prior to the 1860s every Kingsdown house would have had at least one, and sometimes more, servants living in. A householder's social standing could, by and large, be measured by the number of living-in servants, usually including a housemaid, possibly a cook, and a nursemaid if there were young children. The H.O. Wills II family, with their many children, had five at the time of the 1851 census but this was exceptional for Kingsdown.

As the city's population continued to grow, the better-off began to move outwards to the new suburbs. In the dense city centre, however, the living conditions of the poor became more and more intolerable. Bristol lagged badly behind comparable cities in its provision of municipal services and its mortality rate in the middle of the 19th century was third only to Liverpool and Manchester. Provision of drinking water and disposal of waste in the centre was generally little changed since medieval times; typhoid and dysentery were all but endemic among the poor, and in the summer of 1832 cholera reached Bristol. The disease had first arrived in this country only the previous autumn, but had spread rapidly throughout the towns and cities.[16] That year 1,521 cases were reported in Bristol, with 584 deaths, mainly, though not exclusively, among the labouring or poorer classes in the city centre.[17]

In stark contrast to the inner city they overlooked, most of the residents of suburban Kingsdown had access to their own or shared well water and rudimentary drainage, and by the beginning of the 19th century water closets were beginning to replace chamber pots and privies. Overall, living conditions on the King's Down in the early 1800s were relatively good, and an advertisement for a school on Kingsdown Parade said 'Kingsdown air almost insures Health'. By the middle of the century, however, the population in Kingsdown, too, was expanding. The earliest houses were now nearly a hundred years old, cesspools were failing to cope adequately with increased use, and people's sanitary expectations were rising.

A Royal Commission, set up to investigate public health in all large towns, visited Bristol, and its report issued in 1845 makes damning reading.[18] It noted that 'the great mortality of life in Bristol is not to be wondered at when we consider its deficiencies in a sanitary point of view'. One of the two investigators, well-used to such unpleasant situations, found himself unable even to enter one of the alleys in the centre of town because of the overpowering stench from the overflowing privies, and had to stand at the end of the alley and vomit. Conditions in the inner city were dire, but even in more affluent areas, the Commissioners commented, 'ranges of handsome houses … have nothing but a system of cesspools'.

In Kingsdown most of the Georgian houses drained to cesspools, and only some of the later ones were connected to main drains: one ran down Spring Hill, and others to the east down Hillgrove Street, Thomas Street and Nine Tree Hill. But, as these drains discharged their effluent into the Frome via an open ditch between Picton Street in Montpelier and Baptist Mills, they only served to move the problem downhill. The Frome had been diverted into the New Cut in 1825 so the sewage no longer flowed into the enclosed Floating Harbour, but this only partly solved the problem, as most tides did not penetrate far enough upriver to clear all the outpourings. The cesspools serving the majority of the houses were located near to, or even beneath, dwellings and often close to a well providing drinking water for surrounding houses. They leaked into the surrounding soil and needed regular emptying if they were not to overflow. As families became larger, and particularly if water closets were fitted,[19] the constant need to empty the cesspools became an increasing problem.

Five years later, the 1850 Inquiry into the Sewerage, Drainage, Supply of Water and the Sanitary Conditions of the Inhabitants of Bristol, set up following the 1845 Royal Commissioners' report, told in unsparing detail of the unpleasant state of affairs in all parts of the City, including Kingsdown. A selection of their comments and those they received from residents speak for themselves:

> In Dove Street ... there is a drain emptying itself into the middle of said street, the stench arising from which, during the past summer months, was intolerable.

> At one corner of Montague Parade (the west end of Kingsdown Parade) is a house with a cesspool, the contents of which are pumped into the street gutter and produce a very offensive smell. This sewage runs by an open gutter down Montague Hill.

> In Clarence Place ... the drainage is in an exceeding defective state: so much so, that very frequently (especially after rain) the cellars of many of the houses are covered to a depth of several feet with sewage and other filth ... There are two large cesspools directly under some of the houses which are emptied about once a month by means of two pumps causing such an intolerable stench that it is next to impossible to remain in the adjacent houses.

And the owner of Spring Hill House complains

> the [cesspool] behind my house is now quite full and it will take four nights to empty it; part of my tenants are obliged to leave the neighbourhood while it is being removed, from the deadly offensive smell. This cesspool is within four yards of a well of water that supplies about 20 houses.

The inspectors in their Report were equally scathing about Bristol's water supply: 'There are few, if any large towns in England where the supply of water is so inadequate as in Bristol.' They had, however, less cause for complaints on this score in Kingsdown.

Details of the provision of clean water appear in nearly all its 18th-century deeds. A few houses had a single well per plot, others shared rights of way to a well, or had conduits from them connecting to the houses. For instance, an early house in Somerset Street had a well and pump sited in its front area for joint use by neighbours on either side;[20] and four houses on the south side of Kingsdown Parade shared a pipe to a 'spring water well that had lately been sunk' on the opposite side of the Parade,[21] the lead pipe extending 'across those gardens and across Kingsdown Street to a pump made between the underground kitchens of the messuages'.[22] Further, because local well water was extremely hard, many of the houses also had sub-floor reservoirs for collecting rainwater for washing. These cisterns were often capacious: deeds for a house on

Spring Hill mention one beneath the house measuring 9ft 6in long, 5ft 8in wide and 5ft 7in deep.[23]

However, the connection between polluted water and cholera, typhus, typhoid and dysentery was only just beginning to be identified in the second half of the 19th century. And, as the owner of Spring Hill House notes above, there was much potential for pollution of the Kingsdown wells. Furthermore pumps and pipes would frequently clog up and become almost unusable as a result of the local hard water.

Following the Commissioners' reports of 1845 and the later Inquiry of 1850, and with minds concentrated by a second cholera epidemic in 1849 which claimed 778 victims, of whom 444 died,[24] Bristol finally started to improve its public health. It first tackled its water supply, and then set up—despite some local opposition suspicious of civic interference—a Sanitary Commission, which took over jurisdiction of the city's sewers and other services. Water was pumped in from the Mendips, 'not so soft as could be desired, but considerably softer than the waters hitherto in use in the City'. By 1866 the city's Medical Officer of Health was able to report that nearly every house in Bristol was connected to the new supply. At the same time over a hundred miles of sewers were dug throughout the city and connection of house drains with these main sewers proceeded steadily.[25] Those main drains that had continued to empty into the Floating Harbour—34 in 1848—were diverted to discharge downstream of the city into the tidal waters of the Avon.

Succeeding decades saw further investment in Bristol's infrastructure and a growing awareness of the city authorities' civic duty. Investment in servicing the city was coupled with a consolidation of the powers of the various Commissions and Parish Boards. There was increasing professional expertise within the Council, while a series of by-laws against insanitary practices, and their enforcement, meant that Bristol continued to become a cleaner and healthier place.

By 1869 the mortality rate in Bristol had fallen from 28 per 1,000 in 1851 to 22 per 1,000—still very high by today's standards (around 9 per 1,000) but sufficient for *The Times* in October of that year to comment that Bristol had been transformed 'from nearly the most unhealthy to be nearly the most healthy town in Great Britain'.[26]

The 1850 Inquiry had also reported on the maintenance, cleansing and lighting of the Bristol streets, and a year later, and after much negotiation, this too came under the jurisdiction of the Bristol Sanitary Commissioners. Previously, responsibility for the city's infrastructure had rested with a range of authorities both public and private. The Paving Commissioners had been responsible for street and pavement surfaces, local parishes for street cleaning, and one of two private gas companies for street lights. The Commissioners had in their report been very critical of all these services, and particularly of the provision in the out-parishes and suburbs.

In Kingsdown the Georgian developers of the individual houses had had initial responsibility for 'pitching and paving'—the laying of the road setts and pavement—outside that house. Deeds specified that the builder should 'within … the space of one year … pitch or pave or cause to be pitched and paved with stone' their half of the street outside the house. Some even stated that the owners should ensure 'that same railing, pitching and paving shall be for ever hereafter kept in good order and repair'. In practice, Paving Acts of 1749 and 1788 had made the maintenance of public roads and pavements the responsibility of the city, financed through Pitching and Paving parish rates.

The Commissioners nevertheless found that, 'altogether, by whomsoever made or repaired … the highways of [Bristol] are, for the most part, in bad order'. They noted that the outer areas, that is those outside the city boundary, were particularly neglected. The report specifically singled out for criticism the streets in the High Kingsdown area, together with the Back of Kingsdown Parade and Dove Street, while a resident in Portland Street wrote to them in despair: 'I am sorry to say we have no lighting, cleansing, pitching or paving, and yet are within ten minutes of the Exchange.'

Street cleaning and the removal of ashes was the responsibility of the local parishes through the use of 'scavengers', contractors engaged to clean the setted streets and take away the debris twice a week, who were paid for through the parish rates. The Commissioners, however, found that the collection of ashes in the area was also 'not always satisfactory'. In Bristol as a whole there was fair provision for the collection of ashes from the more affluent houses,[27] but parts of the outer parishes and suburbs were often neglected.

Though much of Kingsdown was, it seems, adequately served by the scavengers, the Commissioners comment that, of the 15 streets to the north of the summit, 'only five … are scavenged twice a week, one but seldom and the rest not at all', and they describe a lane at the back of Dove Street where the inhabitants deposited their ashes, 'which are allowed to accumulate to several loads. The scavenger's attention has been drawn to this, but it has not been removed.'

The cleaning of the pavement immediately outside one's house was, however, still the responsibility of the individual householder—though washing down the pavement with a bucket of water and a brush could prove problematic when there was a lack of drains to wash away the slops. In Kingsdown Parade a resident complained that 'the road at the back of Kingsdown Parade … is almost always floating in water, which sometimes runs into the houses; and when the weather dries, it leaves a quantity of filthy mud, which in hot weather is very offensive and unhealthy, and which is left untouched by the scavengers from year to year, who tell us it is not their work to remove it'.

At the time of the 1850 report, street gas lighting in Bristol—then provided by two privately run companies in competition—was also far from perfect. The first gas company in Bristol, using gas made from coal, had been founded in 1815, and the second company, initially using gas made from whale, seal and sometimes vegetable oils, eight years later.[28] At first just a few experimental shops had been gas-lit, then lighting was installed in a public building, Lewins Mead Chapel, and in the main streets.[29] Away from the central areas, though, progress was slow. Even within the city the 1850 report was critical of the general paucity of lights, the irregular distances between them, the often deficient pressure and the high price.

Gas street lighting had begun to reach some of the streets on the slopes of Kingsdown by 1825 but distribution was uneven. Twenty years later the more northern parts of Kingsdown outside of the city boundary—Paul Street, Oxford Street, Portland Street and Clarence Place—are on record as still complaining of unlit streets.

Gas had been installed inside the Methodist Chapel in Portland Street in 1833 and by the late 1830s a few of the Kingsdown houses had changed to the new form of lighting. To the north, most of the new houses of Cotham were built with gas lighting installed.

Over the coming decades the two gas companies expanded their main supplies and improved their service, and in 1853 they amalgamated. Oil had proved to be uneconomic and both were now producing gas from coal. Thirty years later electricity was to become a serious competitor and experiments in electric street lighting were under way in central Bristol as early as 1879. But most Kingsdown houses continued to be lit by gas until the end of the century or the beginning of the next.

During these decades, while the city councils slowly took over responsibility for their citizens' public health and for the provision of basic services, neither they, nor the state in general, played any part in their children's education. To meet this deficit the Church of England and other religious and philanthropic bodies began in the 19th century to set up a system of voluntary elementary education for those who could not afford fee-paying schools; in the private sector a variety of such schools flourished for the middle classes.

There was no compulsion on parents to send their children to school. Indeed in Bristol, according to a paper read to the Bristol Association in 1836, only a quarter of children of school age were actually attending lessons at that time.[30] Furthermore there was no legislation to prevent anyone, however ill-qualified, from opening an educational establishment, and no regulation or inspection of the teaching. Consequently standards across both religious and private schools were extremely variable and the Schools Inquiry Commission of 1864-8 commented that lessons were often 'fragmentary, multifarious, disconnected; taught not scientifically as a subject, but merely as so much information'.

For those Kingsdown residents unable to afford the fees for private education, St James's ran two parochial schools, one at the bottom of Marlborough Hill and one in St James Barton. The Portland Wesleyan Chapel taught children the elements of literacy at Sunday School from 1809 (its day school only opened in 1864), and St Matthew's opened a day school on the corner of Cotham Road South and St Matthew's Road in 1849.

For the Kingsdown middle classes there was a range of private educational establishments, from dame-run day schools for the younger local children to boarding schools with a more regional catchment area. The large family of William Sturge—director of J.P. Sturge, the long-established firm of Bristol land surveyors—who lived in Somerset Street[31] in the 1850s and '60s, probably exemplifies typical local use. When young, their children were educated at home with a governess; they then went to various local dame and day schools and, later, to boarding schools elsewhere in the region.[32]

Entries in the 19th-century street directories show that at least 37 Kingsdown houses, mainly in Kingsdown Parade and Somerset Street, functioned at some time as house-schools, serving local needs at all ages. And at least 32 of these 37 Kingsdown schools offered boarding—probably usually alongside day places—with census returns recording that most of these boarders came from the surrounding counties and Wales.

The schools ranged in size: Mrs and Miss Day, who lived in Kingsdown Parade,[33] advertised in 1865 that, 'assisted by qualified professors', they continued to receive 'a limited number of young ladies to board'. The census of 1861 shows them with just four female boarders, between 11 and 14 years old. In contrast, Mr Vines, at the east end of Somerset Street, aided by two 'competent masters', had 17 male boarders in 1871 and advertised that he took day pupils as well.[34]

The tuition would have been of a variable standard and the subjects taught could range from the academically rigorous mathematics and classics offered by the more ambitious academies to rudimentary reading, writing and scripture, with the obligatory needlework for girls in the dame schools.

It has been noted that in the 1760s, when Mme Gautier opened her school, it offered to teach young ladies French and 'every other branch of polite Education such as fine needlework, writing, dancing, music, etc'. A century later it is unlikely that much would have changed in the education of young women. Elizabeth Sturge says of the Weston-super-Mare boarding school that she went to from 1858 that it had 'the limited curriculum then in vogue' and that 'the result educationally left much to be desired … Lessons having been disposed of in the morning, the afternoons were occupied with needlework and drawing.' The Misses Knott in Devon House, Kingsdown Parade from 1840-4 were also offering French[35]—their sister had just returned from completing her education in France and 'would be teaching French and Italian'—but no other subject on the curriculum is specified.

Schools for boys were usually slightly more rigorous academically. Mr Hill at his Classical and Commercial Academy for Young Gentlemen in Kingsdown Parade at the beginning of the 19th century offered 'English Grammar, Composition and Elocution, Penmanship and Arithmetic, Geography … Astronomy … History and the elements of Mathematics, together with the extras of Languages, Drawing, Music and Dancing'. The Misses Jukes Boarding School for Young Gentlemen in Marlborough House in 1826 offered 'Reading, Orthography, English Grammar and the rudiments of History & Geography'. Writing and arithmetic, Latin, French and drawing were all advertised as extra.

Mr Hill added that Kingsdown air's 'effects, united with domestic regularity, have been repeatedly witnessed in the tender habits of many of the pupils soon quickening into vigour'. The Misses Jukes hinted at a touch of class: each young gentleman was requested to bring a 'Silver Dessert Spoon'!

For older boys born without a silver spoon, the Middle Class Commercial School for boarders and day boys down in King Square trained the numerous clerks familiar from Charles Dicken's novels.[36] Mr Nunn, with his son and 'a full complement of efficient teachers', stated, 'Since the commencement of his Commercial School in 1854 numbers of leading firms and others in the city are annually supplied with boys from his school. His system of teaching writing ensures a fine flowing freehand … The bearing of his boys is manly and genteel.'[37]

English, French, Classical, and Commercial
SCHOOL,
JAMES's-PLACE, Kingsdown, Bristol.

J. HILL presents ackowledgements to his Friends, and respectfully offers to the Public the Terms of his School.

The number of Pupils is limited to 18 Boarders at 21 Guineas per annum, and 1 Guinea entrance, 12 Day-Scholars at 3 Guineas per annum, and Half a Guinea entrance.

FRENCH and LATIN, by the *Rev.* M A. *Desprez.*
DANCING, by *Messrs. Sawier & Baillieu.*
DRAWING, by *J. Hill.*
Each of these Accomplishments 3 Guineas per annum, 10s. 6d. Entrance.

Kingsdown Air almost insures Health. Its effects, united with *domestic regularity*, have been repeatedly witnessed in the tender habits of many of the Pupils soon quickening into vigor.

Such treatment as may produce obedience from respect—not fear—and make business voluntary—not a task—is the discipline of this Seminary.

The School re-opens January 20.

46 *The English, French, Classical and Commercial School run by Mr J. Hill at variously no. 19 Kingsdown Parade (1796) and James's Place (1800). Advertisement,* Felix Farley's Bristol Journal, *1800.*

Late Victorian decades, 1870s–1900s

By the later decades of the 19th century the Georgian suburb of Kingsdown, its terraces now less highly valued, saw change in both its physical and social make-up. New houses built during these decades were mainly smaller terraced houses, infilling between the larger Georgian houses on the contours,[38] or stepping boldly up the hill in one-time gardens.[39] The grand Observatory House,[40] seen at the eastern end of Somerset Street in Booth's picture of 1819 (fig. 44), was demolished *c*.1885 and four houses built on its site.[41]

The 1860s and '70s saw the move by the more affluent middle classes from Kingsdown to Cotham and beyond beginning to gather momentum. By the last quarter of the century the census shows that several of the houses, previously occupied by single families with one or two servants living in, were in multiple occupation, or housing families who took in lodgers to help pay the rent. Many families were now without any live-in servants at all and many of the larger houses were in institutional or commercial use.

In Somerset Street the former Wills family home became in 1884 the Bristol Industrial School for Girls, supported by voluntary donations and government allowance.[42] It housed around sixty 'destitute and vagrant girls of the Protestant persuasion', who received three hours of daily instruction in reading, writing and geography, daily religious instruction and training in washing, cooking, needlework and housework.

In Kingsdown Parade James Lockier's grand house was, from 1890 until the 1930s, the Institution for Deaf Children, catering for the education of 'deaf mute' pupils and financed by the School Board.[43]

Marlborough House, on Marlborough Hill, the 'mansion' of David and Jane Jones in the earliest days of Kingsdown, which had been home to the Misses Jukes' Preparatory Boarding School for Young Gentlemen, was as early as 1837 a Boys' Remand Home. By 1871 it was the home of the Refuge Society for Girls, set up 'for the same benevolent purposes as the penitentiary ... the inmates ... employed in washing and needlework'.[44]

In King Square, too, the houses occupied in Georgian times by Latimer's 'several wealthy families' now housed institutions and workshops. One house was from 1822-33 the Bristol Medical School,[45] founded to provide instruction for those who 'walked the wards' in the nearby hospital and the predecessor of the later Faculty of Medicine at Bristol University. A second in the 1850s-80s housed the 'Middle Class Commercial School' mentioned previously,[46] while another was bought by the city council in 1877 and fitted out as a branch library for the

47 *(Top and bottom) Llewellin's Machine Co., advertisement in* The Graphic, *1885.*

northern parts of the city.[47] The east side housed a wholesale boot and shoe manufacturer,[48] and in a workshop behind one of the houses on the north side the engineering firm of Llewellin's started life in 1883, expanding into the two neighbouring buildings later in the century.[49]

Llewellin's, founded by William Maberley Llewellin,[50] an inventor and patent agent, initially made clocks and time-recording machines, but later moved to the production of gears of all types and sizes. The business continues successfully today, producing a wide range of specialist gears for process plants and engineering establishments, as well as for vintage cars and traction engines.

One of the most striking changes in British society during these later decades of the century was in the position of women: in their occupations, in their role in public and political life, and in their education.

The growing belief that a married 'woman's place is in the home' permeated down through all social classes. The number of employed married women (with husbands alive) fell nationally from 1 in 4 in 1851 to 1 in 10 in 1911, and in Kingsdown the area census returns in the decades 1851-91 show that despite the change in social class of residents by the end of that period, there are almost no working wives.

With regard to single women, in contrast, there was a profound shift

in the expectations of the public role they might play and a consequent expansion of the things it was considered 'respectable' for an unmarried middle-class woman to do. The Kingsdown census returns show increasing numbers of unmarried daughters, single women and younger widows becoming teachers, governesses and lady's companions, being employed as dressmakers or milliners, or serving in confectionery or drapers shops.

There was also in late 19th-century Britain the early beginnings of a feminist agenda—and Bristol, it has been said, possessed one of the most impressive early women's movements in the country.[51] This came in particular from the single female members of nonconformist professional families. All were actively seeking to improve the lot of the disadvantaged in society and challenge the virtual exclusion of women from public life and national politics. The daughters of Kingsdown were well represented in the movement: three Quaker sisters, Emily, Elizabeth and Helen Sturge, and their Anglican childhood friend and neighbour Mary Clifford (the daughter of the Rev. J.B. Clifford, the first vicar of St Matthew's Church), who had all spent their childhood in Somerset Street, worked tirelessly for the feminist cause.[52]

Emily Sturge was the youngest member of the Bristol School Board, formed in 1870, and was active in lobbying for women's suffrage. In 1881 she helped found and, with her sister Helen, actively supported the Bristol Women's Liberal Association, which 'diffused knowledge on political questions … among the women of Bristol'. The third sister, Elizabeth, was involved in Mary Carpenter's pilot Reformatory School for Girls at Red Lodge and also worked for the welfare of female factory workers and the provision of good housing.

Mary Clifford was one of the first four women in Bristol to become a Poor Law Guardian, in which capacity she was particularly involved in improving the conditions in the workhouse and the lot of pauper children. The appointment of women as Guardians, though it was to prove a popular move when put to the vote, was strongly resisted by many of the male establishment. Elizabeth Sturge describes how, out canvassing for her childhood neighbour, she was 'literally turned out of doors by an old clergyman on whom [she] called to ask for his vote!' Later, Mary was also an active member, and for several years president, of the National Council of Women, which promoted the need for better housing and education for the poor.

Education in Kingsdown, for most of its less affluent residents, continued to be provided by voluntary agencies until the beginning of the next century. The Education Bill of 1870 implied for the first time that the government had a responsibility to ensure elementary education was available for all children in England and Wales, and slowly over the decades successive bills increased the state's authority. School attendance was made compulsory up to the age of 10 in 1880 and from 1891 state education finally became free for all pupils. However, Bristol, as so often, was slow to act.

The Bristol School Board, set up in 1871, judged the Kingsdown area to be so well provided for by the voluntary sector that for another thirty years they deemed Board School unnecessary, preferring to provide grants to the existing voluntary aided schools. During these years the thousand or so local girls and boys were served by three Church of England schools, one Methodist and one Ragged School: St Matthew's School in Cotham Road South, St Michael's School, St James Parochial School, the Portland Wesleyan Day School in Portland Street, and the St James's Ragged School, which provided education for destitute children at the bottom of Marlborough Hill. Only the Ragged School was totally government supported and therefore free for its pupils; the Portland Chapel in 1903 charged its 300 children a total of £360 a year, which was supplemented at that date by a total government grant of £310, and St Matthew's was probably similar.

After 1880 there was in addition the Truants' School on the corner of Southwell Street and Horfield Road for those boys who regularly failed to attend school after attendance became compulsory. They would be taught there for the time necessary to cure their habit, and the school seems to have served its purpose well for in 1883/4 it was commended by government inspectors for producing excellent results. The boys 'became some of the most regular attenders when they returned to their normal school', though there is no description of how this was achieved.

While the number of church school places in the area had increased since the early and mid-Victorian decades, the number of private schools, particularly those for girls, had decreased. This was partly a result of Kingsdown's change in social make-up, and partly an increasing awareness of the need for middle-class females to learn more than needlework and other such arts. It resulted in a significant drop in the number of small, private, non-academic, schools for girls by the final decades of the 19th century. Although some of the larger private boys' schools were still operating in the area, and a new boys' preparatory and boarding school had just opened at the east end of Kingsdown Parade,[53] only three girls' schools are mentioned, one of these in Kingsdown Parade ambitiously calling itself Kingsdown High School for Girls.[54] Many of the daughters of the new residents of Cotham and Redland could expect to go to

Redland High School for Girls, which opened in 1882, or Colston Girls' School, which opened in 1891, in order to gain qualifications more relevant for the age.

Throughout these years the gross deficiencies of the earlier educational 'system' were alleviated in part by numerous opportunities for adult self-improvement: public libraries, educational lectures and learned societies were all taken up by a population eager for self-advancement.

Figures collated in 1889 for the North District Library in King Square showed over 74,000 books being borrowed a year.[55] To the west, along the contour, Bristol's University College opened in 1876 offering numerous well-attended courses and lectures. The older Sturge daughters, conscious of their inadequate early education, attended 'Lectures for Ladies' there and studied mathematics and sciences as well as arts subjects. Science was also taught locally in Kingsdown Parade, where from 1847 to the end of the century there was the Bristol School of Chemistry, under the tutelage of the impressively qualified Dr Griffin. The laboratory was open daily for research or instruction and courses of lectures were given at intervals in the classroom.[56] An 1835 advertisement for one of Dr Griffin's courses stated that it was 'An introduction to Chemical Science Serviceable to all engaged in Industrial Pursuits' and adds that they were 'sufficiently clear and popular to prove attractive to Ladies and Young Persons'.[57]

In the 1880s the city council recognised that, as the authority for public health, it also had a civic duty to provide for the well-being of its citizens and provided facilities for physical exercise and recreation, including public swimming baths. Kingsdown, in common with other middle-class areas such as Clifton, Hotwells and Montpelier, already had a private pool, the Royal Baths, built sometime prior to 1880 by a Mr Popham, on a site now part of High Kingsdown.[58] There was also a gymnasium, and in 1887 a fund-raising 'Assault-at-Arms' was held there by the Bicycle and Tricycle Club, which included boxing matches, fencing and a tug-of-war.[59] Though private, the baths were used by the city's elementary schools and their annual swimming competition, promoted by the Bristol Humane Society, was held there.[60] When, in 1897, the Royal Baths came onto the market, it was considered eminently sensible for the Bristol Bath Committee to purchase them and they remained a well-used place of recreation for schools and locals for the next 70 years.

FOUR

War and Peace

The 20th century continued Bristol's progress as a successful—if not particularly dynamic—city. Its economy gradually shifted from one largely dependent on a traditional base, including heavy engineering, trade and commerce, to one encompassing high technology, financial and legal services.

The extension of the tramway system prior to the Second World War and the increasing acquisition by its citizens of motor cars in the 1930s led to a large expansion of Bristol's residential area. Over 36,000 new homes, both private and council-owned, were built between the wars, and the city almost doubled in area. Most of this new growth was on the outskirts: industrial development began to move from the centre and the greater part of the new housing was built on the outer edges of the city.

Even before the war much of Kingsdown's housing was shabby and in need of extensive maintenance and restoration, and Hitler's bombs caused further damage. By the time peace finally came, major repair of Kingsdown's physical state was very necessary. There was throughout the country a strong mood for a brave new fairer world, in which inner-city 'slums' were to be cleared and residents rehoused, but the people of Kingsdown, resenting such a perceived slur on their homes, fought the authorities for the following twenty years, with lesser or greater success.

1900–39

There were only two new buildings of note within Kingsdown during these years: Kingsdown Council School on the summit of the Down,[1] and the King Edward VII block of the Bristol Royal Infirmary at the foot of Marlborough Hill.

Kingsdown School opened in Southwell Street in 1910. Up to the beginning of the 20th century the education of children in the area had, as previously noted, been mainly in the hands of the voluntary or the independent sector. In 1902, Bristol's newly created Local Education

48   *Kingsdown School, Southwell Street, Loxton, c. 1910.*

49   *The houses and shops on Upper Maudlin Street prior to demolition in the early 20th century for the new hospital building.*

50   *King Edward VII Memorial Building, Upper Maudlin Street, c.1915.*

Authority finally took over responsibility for education in the area and eight years later the children of St Matthew's and Portland Schools were transferred to a new 600-pupil elementary school, Kingsdown School. St James's Ragged School, at the bottom of Marlborough Hill,[2] and St Michael's School, by the church, both became primary schools at this time. The Industrial School continued in Ashley House until 1918.

The King Edward VII extension to the Bristol Royal Infirmary, which opened in 1912 on the Lower Montagues area, was the first incursion of the hospital into Kingsdown. It was designed by a renowned architect of the time, Charles Holden, and his partner Percy Adams. Built around and added to since, it is difficult today to fully appreciate its fine qualities, though it was originally an exemplar of new thinking in medicine and also seen as an important step towards an architecture of the 20th century. On its northern side were large balconies providing light, air and views to the wards, and terraced gardens (now built over) where convalescent patients could stroll. Funded by public appeal, its mission when it opened in 1912 was to 'treat the poor'. When war broke out two years later though, it was temporarily offered to the nation by the people of Bristol to treat the wounded soldiers of the First World War.

The public appeal for the extension of the hospital had been spearheaded by Sir George White (1854-1916),[3] the transport entrepreneur, who

51 *St Michael's Buildings off Paul Street, birthplace of George White, 1854.*

donated generously himself. Sir George had been born in modest circumstances in Kingsdown, in a small court off Paul Street, the fourth child of a painter/decorator and a one-time domestic servant. Educated at St Michael's School, he became a junior clerk in a law firm whose clients were involved in tramway promotion. The gifted entrepreneur soon saw the potential for developing the technology further. To acquire the necessary capital he set up his own stockbroking firm in the centre of Bristol and worked for 10 years building up funds and making the necessary business contacts, before playing an increasingly important and successful role in the Bristol Tramway Company. Later he diversified into motor buses, taxis and trains, and perhaps his most lasting achievement was the establishment of the British and Colonial Aeroplane Company in 1910. The company initially produced bi-planes which, though intended for civilian passenger transport, were to play a key role in the First World War. After a series of business moves, the B&C Aeroplane Company became a part of British Aerospace; it is now BAE Systems, still one of Bristol's major manufacturing and international companies.

52   *Drill at St Michael's Hill House: 6th Battalion Glos. Regt HQ.*

The First World War was to see many Kingsdown men serving with the Sixth Gloucesters, a volunteer battalion founded locally in 1900. Initially drilling took place in a variety of sites including, in the winter months, Kingsdown Baths, its floor heavily covered in sawdust. Lectures were given in local schoolrooms. However, in November that year a large Georgian house at the top of St Michael's Hill, the present site of the maternity hospital, was purchased by the regiment. Drill could now take place in the converted garden and was carried out in the evening after ordinary working hours, with 'special arrangements made to suit night workers'. Two of the Sixth's three regiments fought in the First World War, the third being part of the home reserves. They fought in Flanders, France and Italy, gaining 15 honours but losing over 800 men in battle.

Though houses and shops had been cleared for the building of the King Edward VII block on the Lower Montagues, there remained elsewhere in Kingsdown a strong and vibrant community. Kingsdown residents saw themselves not as a suburb but as a self-contained 'village'. Within the confines of Kingsdown they could literally be provided for from the cradle to the grave. Their babies could be delivered either at home

53 *A board listing the shops and services available in Kingsdown and St Michael's Hill in 1939, prepared for the Kingsdown '250' City Museum exhibition.*

Shops & Services

'It was a village in itself: it was a hive of industry and you could buy anything here in the 30's ' - Arthur Tuck, the newsagent.

Some of the shops and services available in Kingsdown in 1939

F. R. WARLOW
M.P.S.
Chemist,
COTHAM RD, SOUTH
For . . . . CAREFUL DISPENSING
and
BEST STOCKS OF PATENT MEDICINES,
DRUGS, PHOTOGRAPHIC, TOILET and
WIRELESS REQUISITES.

W. G. HODDINOTT
3, CHRISTMAS STEPS
& 52, COLSTON STREET.
Groceries & Provisions
Speciality
MATTERSONS FAMOUS BACON,
DEVONSHIRE BUTTER.
AND AND NOTED TEAS.

H. CAISH
Baker and Confectioner,
U?a Parties, Socials, etc.
catered for.
Deliveries to all parts -
Kingsdown Bakery, Paul St.,
Telephone 50058.

V. F. RICHARDS
Late F. F. WHITE.
*Newsagent : Stationer,
Tobacconist : Confectioner.*
42 ALFRED PLACE, KINGSDOWN
BRISTOL.
*Morning and Evening Newspapers
and all Periodicals regularly delivered.*

F OR
MILLINERY,
DRAPERY of every description
LOWEST PRICES.

T RY
F.E. CALCUTT
144 ST MICHAEL'S HILL,
BRISTOL.

GODFREYS
Specialists in
DAINTY FANCIES for Afternoon Teas
also CAKES BREAD ROLLS, Etc.
Bishopston Bakery, 239 Gloucester Rd.
Also at 140 ST. MICHAEL'S HILL COTTHAM
and 51 HORFIELD MARKET, FILTON.
BRISTOL.

Telephone 33161.
H. WINTER
Colston Fish &
Poultry Supply
ENGLISH RABBITS A SPECIALITY
Special Terms to Restaurants,
Hotels, Canteens, &c.
COLSTON ST.,
St. Michael's.

Paul Street
3 greengrocers
2 general stores
3 boot repairers
a grocer
a tobacconist
a butcher
a pork butcher
a clothes dealer
a beer retailer
a motorcar body builder
a baker
a farrier
a confectioners
a coal dealer
a draper
a hairdresser

Oxford Street
a confectioner
2 chimney sweeps
a window cleaner
a dairy

Clevedon Terrace
a greengrocer
a confectioners
a grocer
a Post Office

Kingsdown Parade
a fine arts publisher
a laundry
a general stores
a grocer
a bakery
a garage
a greengrocer & fruit
a fish & chip shop
The Co-op

Somerset Street
a general stores
a greengrocer
a draper

Cotham Road South
a chemist
a milliner
2 grocers
a confectioner
a dairy
a plumber
a draper
a beer retailer
a greengrocer

Alfred Place
a grocers & greengrocers
a fish & chip shop
a newsagent
a barber
a boot repairer
the Express shoe service
an oil & colour man
2 general stores
a pie dealer
a grocer
a confectioner
2 fishmongers

Top of Horfield Road
an umbrella maker
a general stores
a butcher
a tobacconist
a cycle accessories store
a boot repairer
a newsagent
a greengrocer
a grocer

L. WILSON
High-Class Purveyor,
40, MARLBOROUGH STREET
ST. JAMES.
Families Waited upon Daily for Orders.
A TRIAL SOLICITED.

J. H. EVANS & SONS
Masons and Builders.
Building Ranges, Stoves and Grates of
all Descriptions fixed on the most
Approved principles. All Sanitary
Matters under Personal Attention.
HOUSE REPAIRS IN GENERAL.
HORFIELD RD., ST. MICHAEL'S

F. T. HALLIER
Oil, Colour, Tinware
and General Hard-
ware Stores.
Telephone 333596.
143, ST. MICHAEL'S HILL

P. BISHOP
36 Alfred Place, Kingsdown
Fresh Fish and Vegetables
Daily.
Families Waited ORDERS
on Daily DELIVERED

TELEPHONE 50845.
W. D. MEEK,
COTHAM ROAD DAIRY,
7, COTHAM ROAD SOUTH.
High Class Dairy Produce.
Rich New Milk and Butter
direct from Local Farms
Fresh Butter . New-laid Eggs a Speciality.
Raw and Cooked Cream made Fresh Daily.

H. B. BURT
General Hardware Stores
3 & 5, ALFRED PLACE,
KINGSDOWN, BRISTOL.
Drains, Tea and Toilet Sets, Large Assortment,
Lowest Prices.
Earthenware Lot out to Hire.
Large Stock of Paints, Enamels, Brushes, Oils,
Churchware, etc.
ESTABLISHED 1887.
A. H. JONES
Dairyman, Greengrocer, &c.
27, St. Michael's Hill (near) Bristol
FAMILIES SUPPLIED AT THEIR RESIDENCES
WITH MILK, CREAM, BUTTER, EGGS, AND
FRESH VEGETABLES DAILY.
Telephone 83061.
The Acme Press
Printers, Publishers and
Advertising Contractors.
7a PAUL St, KINGSDOWN, BRISTOL
Paper Bags, Grease Proof
Wrapping Paper O Merchants.

Telephone No. 23949. Fifty Years' Reputation. Estimates on Application.
WOOD & CO. Complete Undertakers, Funeral Carriage and Motor Hearse Proprietors.
Note the Only Address:
Office and Residence: 10, PERRY ROAD, PARK ROW, BRISTOL.
Workshop and Carriage Department: KINGSDOWN PARADE.
FUNERALS, WITH MOTOR HEARSE AND BROUGHAM, COMPLETE FROM $7 10s.
MOTOR HEARSES FOR THE CONVEYANCE OF BODIES TO ANY PART OF THE COUNTRY.

or, after 1914, at the Bristol Maternity Hospital, which had opened immediately opposite its present site; and in death they could be buried in a coffin made by Wood's, the funeral directors who had a workshop and stables in Kingsdown Parade.[4] In between these milestones, as Arthur Tuck, who moved from Paul Street to set up the eponymous newsagency in Cotham Road South in the '30s, recalled, 'Kingsdown ... was a hive of industry and you could buy anything here.' There was a large Co-op at the end of the Parade selling groceries, confectionery, drapery, clothing and boots (and with a dancehall holding regular tea dances on its first floor).[5] Most Kingsdown streets also had their own small grocery and greengrocery stores. The dairy in Oxford Street delivered milk to the houses in a handcart, while the one on the corner of Somerset Street and Fremantle Road still carried it in pails hung from a yoke across the shoulder. Paul Street was a small thriving shopping centre where you could buy food from a choice of three greengrocers, a grocer, a butcher, a pork butcher, a baker and many others. You could buy a dress, have your hair done and your boots repaired (or, if you were well off, your carriage). And if you couldn't find what you wanted, then there was another equally flourishing 'village' just round the corner on St Michael's Hill. There was even, briefly, a bank on the corner of Clevedon Terrace to handle all this commerce.

54 *The Cotham Co-op, 1906-65, from* A study in Democracy: Industrial Co-operation in Bristol *by Edward Jackson. The building's original owners can still be identified today from the clasped hands in the building's ornate plaster and stonework, together with the beehive, the sheaf of corn on the plaques on the façade, and the pineapples, gourds and ears of corn around the windows.*

55 *No. 36 Somerset Street was 'Prossers' from 1889 to 1966. Initially a dairy, then a grocers and, for a while, also an undertakers, it was run by Richard and Blanche Prosser and later by their daughters. By the 1960s, as the houses on the slopes below crashed down, Miss Lilian Prosser, now in her 80s, was running the place herself. 'Walk in please, walk out pleased' said the faded card on the door, and inside, with her Victorian gas brackets, large tea caddies with gilt lettering, and beam scales with copper pans hung on chains, Miss Prosser remained a welcome, if anachronistic, sign of stability for Kingsdown residents.*

Further local employment was provided in King Square by Llewellin's Gears, Comac the boot and shoe manufacturer, and, on the summit of the Down, Parker's Bakery and the Bristol District Laundry. Parker's was originally housed on the corner of Kingsdown Parade and Clevedon Terrace, but took advantage of cheap prices and lack of planning enforcement in the 1930s and '40s to buy up and demolish house after house on the north side of the Parade. By 1950 the sites of

56 *Kingsdown Carriage Works, 40-2 Paul Street, c.1908. The carriage works was first set up in 1882, coming under the proprietorship of J. Ford four years later. He was succeeded in 1931 by his son J. Ford Jnr who, aware of modern trends, promptly changed the works to 'Motor Car Body Builders'. It remained as such until 1966, when most of Paul Street was demolished to form High Kingsdown.*

six houses and gardens in Kingsdown Parade contained their factory and its yard for horse-drawn delivery carts.[6] Similarly, across the road, the Bristol District Laundry had in 1922 taken over the laundry on the corner of St Matthew's Road and Clevedon Terrace, and in 1933 had expanded into the early Georgian house next door, using it to store sheets in, and its garden to accommodate their new boiler in a corrugated shed with a 40ft chimney.[7]

No community is immune to events outside its boundaries, however, and across the Channel there was increasing political turbulence as aggressive dictators engaged in unprovoked attacks. In the early summer of 1937 Kingsdown residents had a taste of one of the consequences of war when no. 10 Kingsdown Parade, no longer the Institution for Deaf Children and now empty, became home for a year to some forty Basque children from the Bilbao region of Spain and their carers.

The children were temporary refugees from the Spanish Civil War. Bilbao had declared for the left-wing Republicans at the start of the war and, following the destruction by aerial bombing of nearby Guernica, parents in the area, fearing further such attacks, evacuated some 25,000 of their children. Nearly 4,000 of them came to Britain; others went largely to France, but also to Belgium, Switzerland, Mexico and the Soviet Union. The British evacuees were initially housed in tents near Southampton and then, following a wide appeal for aid by the organisers, in small 'colonies' (*colonias*) around the country—including the one in Kingsdown Parade. A year later though, Franco having captured all northern Spain, an uneasy peace returned to the Bilbao area and it gradually became safe for the homesick children to return to their families.[8]

Another refugee from fascism, Klaus Fuchs, was living further down the Parade while he studied for a PhD in physics at the University, having been forced, as a member of the German Communist Party, to flee from Germany after the Nazis gained power in 1933. He was in lodgings that were also home during the pre-war years to two other physics graduates, Cecil Powell and Allan Nunn May.[9] All three were left-wing pacifists and committed in their different ways to a search for world peace. Powell, awarded the Nobel Prize for Physics in 1950, spent much of his life campaigning against the danger of nuclear weapons and advocating the peaceful use of science. Nunn May and Fuchs were imprisoned in 1946 and 1950 respectively for (independently) passing information to the Russians on Britain and America's atomic bomb research programmes, Nunn May because he felt it was 'a contribution I could make to the safety of mankind', Fuchs because of his belief in the Communist movement as a way forward.

The Second World War: The Blitz

The Second World War saw Bristol playing an important role in the country's defences and in the manufacture of aircraft and, to a lesser extent, of warships. In addition, after the USA joined the fray Bristol provided a key port for the landing of American troops and supplies, while Clifton College became the UK headquarters of the United States 1st Army. Inevitably, the city was a target for bombing raids by the German Luftwaffe, with the first recorded bomb on Bristol falling in June 1940 and with major attacks, particularly on the two aircraft manufacturing plants and the port facilities, continuing through 1940 and 1941. In all 1,299 Bristolians were killed and another 1,303 seriously injured. Some 9,000 buildings were destroyed, or had to be demolished, and much of the city's centre—just below Kingsdown—was destroyed.

The residents of Kingsdown had a nervous grandstand view of the burning city during enemy raids. As in cities throughout the land, those left behind settled down to the privations of the war years and learnt to live with the threat of death. At the western end the rambling cellars of one of the early Georgian houses were reinforced to provide a small public air-raid shelter,[10] though most residents preferred to remain in their own basements, under-stair cupboards or garden shelters. No. 10 Kingsdown Parade, no longer home to the Basque children, became a warden's post. The younger pupils of Kingsdown School were evacuated to Devon and Cornwall.

Several residents lost their lives. One Alfred Place family made the local headlines when their house received a direct hit with the family of seven sheltering in the cellar. The husband and the youngest child were killed outright, but the five other members, including the very pregnant wife, were trapped under the rubble. It took the best part of the day, with rescuers, including the matron and sister of the maternity hospital, working in extremely perilous conditions, to get them all safely out. Mother and baby survived and the maternity staff were awarded the George Cross for their brave work.[11]

At the foot of the hill, King Square was badly damaged by bombs, losing both the boot and shoe factories and several of its houses. At the western end of the summit part of the *Montague Inn*, the warden's post, another house further along the Parade and the houses on either side of Alfred Place were hit.[12] St Michael's House, home of the Sixth, was destroyed, as were their quarters at Colston Fort on Montague Place, ending their association with Kingsdown.[13] At the eastern end the first six houses of Fremantle Road were victims of a high-explosive bomb.[14] To the north many of the shops and houses in Paul Street were razed to the ground, and throughout Kingsdown houses suffered damage from shrapnel and incendiary bombs.

57 *The Royal Gloucestershire Hussars D Squadron, September 1939, at the Colston Fort, their headquarters until it was blitzed in 1941.*

The Post-War Years: *Kingsdown Under Threat*

While hostilities were still waging, Britain had been planning its brave new world, one where health, welfare, education and fit housing were the right of all. When peace finally came there was, throughout the country, a strong mood for change and for just such a fairer society. The new Labour government started to implement Bevan's welfare state: grants were to be given to local authorities for replacement of their slums, the National Health Service was founded, and state education was to be expanded at all levels. The 1947 Planning Act required Bristol and other cities to produce a plan for land use within their area for the next 20 years, with a remit to secure a proper balance between the inevitably competing demands for land and the wider public interest.

The Kingsdown area, the Bristol Royal Infirmary to its south and Bristol University to the west, with many of its houses in disrepair, was extremely vulnerable. When in 1952 Bristol finally produced its Development Plan, residents found that large areas of Kingsdown and St Michael's Hill were considered suitable for the building of new homes, and the physical expansion of both the University and the Hospital.

Initially around sixty acres of land on St Michael's Hill and Kingsdown were set aside for these purposes. The University zone was to be to the west of St Michael's Hill, the Hospital zone to the east of St Michael's Hill across to Marlborough Hill, and the public

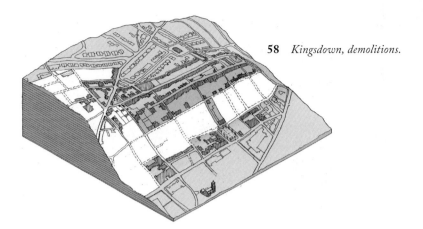

58 *Kingsdown, demolitions.*

housing zone the land on the lower Kingsdown slopes and the area now occupied by High Kingsdown. In addition, the area occupied by Kingsdown Secondary School, since 1949 a secondary modern, was to be increased and space reserved for a new primary school.[15]

Kingsdown was still a strong community but its houses were at best shabby, at worst derelict. It was some two hundred years since they had been built and they were in need of expensive maintenance and installation of basic services considered necessary in the 20th century. In 1955 housing officers began to identify those houses likely to be deemed 'unfit for human habitation', somewhat reminiscent of the Victorian Public Health Commissioners' assessment a hundred years earlier. Rumour was rife as local people speculated on the possible extent of demolition, their unease exacerbated by the city council's reluctance to give out any official information. They justified this by pointing out that Whitehall would in any case have the final say. With planning uncertainty causing blight throughout the area, the decline that had started before the war gathered speed.

The 1947 Act also required the city to draw up a list of 'buildings of special architectural interest', though even this would not necessarily provide protection. The only Kingsdown houses proposed were Devon House (no. 34a) and no. 25 in Kingsdown Parade, nos 23-4 and 26-9 in Somerset Street, the 18th-century houses in King Square, Harford House in Dighton Street, and five houses in Blenheim Square (subsequently demolished for the BRI development).[16] The politics behind some of the inclusions and exclusions can only be guessed at.

At first the city council attempted to play down local fears that the area might be swept away. In 1956 the local paper (in an article by 19-year-old reporter and playwright-to-be Tom Stoppard) quoted the planning committee as saying that 'about 20 buildings were likely to be destroyed in the none too distant future'. Though there might be

59 'The houses were at best shabby, at worst derelict.' Anti-clockwise from left: Paul Street, north side, 1960s; Spring Hill, c.1964; Dove Street, early 1960s; and Oxford Street, east side, 1965.

others, 'no further plans have been made up till now' and 'fears for the suburb are likely to turn out to be unfounded, or very nearly so'.[17]

The uncertainty continued throughout 1957 and '58, with consequent decay throughout the whole area. By March 1958 the City's Housing Manager reported that there were 151 unfit buildings in the area between Duke Street and Dove Street, and 64 in the area which included St Michael's Hill and the streets now incorporated into High Kingsdown. This represented some three-quarters of the total housing stock in those areas.

Despite this, many residents and well-wishers remained determined that Kingsdown could and would be saved and to this end, in 1957, they formed the Kingsdown and St Michael's Area Protection Association.[18] While not denying that some of the houses in the streets under threat were almost derelict, the protestors argued that retaining and restoring them would result in a more attractive and, they felt, cheaper solution than demolition and replacement. Feelings ran high. At a well-attended public meeting in September 1958 the chairman of the housing committee reported that letters he had received described the council's plans for clearance of the unfit houses as being 'a manoeuvre of the Socialist party of Bristol to obtain control of the land', which he denied. Residents spoke movingly on the pleasures of living in Kingsdown in houses many had occupied all their lives and objected strongly when the term 'slum clearance' was used. A man in the audience complained, 'The term slum clearance is a slur on Kingsdown. Kingsdown is not a slum.' The chairman of the housing committee apologised: 'We use these words because they are in the Act of Parliament. We never use them in any derogatory sense … What we want is an area with decent houses fit for people to live in.'[19]

The local press reported at length and in great detail, and the *Manchester Guardian*,[20] the *Observer*,[21] and the *Architectural Review* also devoted columns to the Kingsdown story. Well-known public figures championing the cause included John Betjeman, the poet and author ('this airy suburb, this place of Georgian view … Such a unique district can never be replaced'),[22] and Ian Nairn, the respected architectural critic: 'England's only vertical suburb … nowhere else [in Britain] is there an 18th century suburb apparently hanging in mid-air over a big city.'[23] The Royal Fine Art Commission stated that they 'would like to see as many as possible of the existing buildings in the area preserved in any redevelopment that may be found necessary'.

The response by officers to such comments by national figures was generally defensive, with councillors unable to understand why Kingsdown provoked such excitement. The chairman of the housing committee, in the face of a hostile audience at a public meeting, said, 'I admit people have said certain things about Kingsdown—people who go into high and fulsome praise about Kingsdown—but they do not live here.'

That the councillors and their officers should feel maligned was not surprising. They aspired, as they had said, to provide a better life for their citizens, including 'decent and fit' housing, even though, to our eyes, their confidence in the way they might achieve this seemed somewhat misplaced. In their view, demolition and new build was the only solution, not the restoration of 200-year-old houses, which they argued would, contrary to the campaigners' arguments, be financially unrealistic. In March 1958 it was announced that compulsory purchase orders would be sought for large parts of the Kingsdown and St Michael's Hill area. Later that year the city council published plans for the redevelopment on the slopes, followed by plans for the streets now incorporated into High Kingsdown. It was to be a new Kingsdown, 'of which future Bristolians will feel very proud'. It would feature 20th-century architecture and planning principles designed to harmonise with the buildings that were being retained (i.e. Kingsdown Parade, Somerset Street and Alfred Place), but would in no way try to copy Georgian architecture. As a councillor said, 'We must have an architecture of our own and not try to copy that of the past, however good it may have been.'

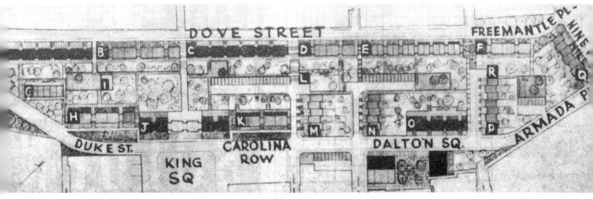

60a   *The 1958 proposals for the Dove Street/Duke Street area* (Western Daily Press, *14 October 1958*).

Announcing his plans for the slopes in July, the city architect told the committee, 'I come here this morning with no ideas for skyscraper flats.' Rather, the proposed design consisted of blocks of flats and maisonettes, most of four to five storeys, running along Dove Street and Duke Street, together with several three-storey ones along the frontages to Thomas, Gay and Hillgrove Streets. The existing road pattern would be used in the main, but with some new link roads. In total, 293 dwellings were to be provided, a similar density to the houses being replaced.

In November 1958 his scheme for the High Kingsdown area was announced: a single eight-storey block of flats near Kingsdown Baths and small blocks of three and five storeys, also 'echoing Georgian layout but modern in design' and 'set among paved and grassed courtyards with plenty of trees'.

The local authority approved both schemes, as later, with minor modifications, did the Royal Fine Arts Commission, and a three-day public inquiry in December 1958 about the site clearance found against the hundred or more objectors. However, as the chairman of the planning committee had warned at an earlier meeting, Bristol were not masters in their own household and Whitehall had the final say. There had been large increases in population after the war, a million extra children being born in the five years following. The government was under pressure to produce more homes and councils were consequently being encouraged

61   *The 1958 proposals for the High Kingsdown area (*Bristol Evening Post, *25 November 1958).*

DOVE Sᵀ

KING SQUARE

62 *The 1962 proposals for the Dove Street/Duke Street 16 storey flats (*Bristol Evening Post, *2 September 1962)*

63 *The flats as built at 14 storeys (*Bristol Evening Post, *4 October 1967)*

to build at ever greater densities, and in 1958 central government announced a subsidy for every floor over five storeys. So the Ministry of Housing rejected the council's plans because they were of 'too low density'—and without ministerial approval Bristol would get no housing grants.

In 1962 Bristol presented a new plan for the lower slopes: three 16-storey slab blocks at right angles to the hillside, reduced in height the following year to 14 storeys after considerable public protest, separated by six-storey terraces along the contour.

Over the following months the 18th-century houses on the lower slopes were demolished and three years later work started on the site, cutting a swathe through the historic street pattern. In 1967 the first occupants of 'Lower' Kingsdown moved in. As a gesture to the site's earlier history, the blocks of flats had been named after some of the terraces they replaced: instead of the three- and four-storey brick terraces of Carolina Row, Fremantle Place and Armada Place there were now 14-storey concrete blocks called Carolina House, Fremantle House and Armada House.

Today the flats still feel inappropriate in their context, and pre-clearance photographs of 1960 recording the empty, but not derelict, houses on the

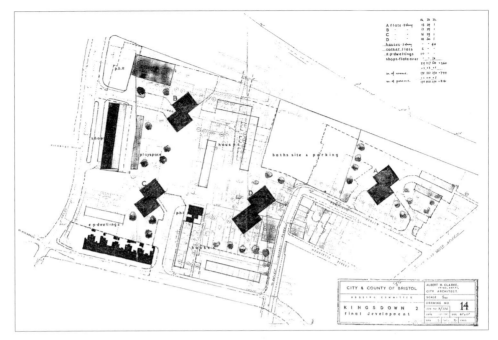

64   *High Kingsdown No. 2 planning application 1965/6.*

site, make for rueful viewing. It is hard to regard this development in the terms described in the Bristol City newsletter of 1968:

> The development is imposing without obtruding aggressively against the skyline. On a fine day, when the slender blocks are crisply etched against the sky, sunlight and shadow emphasise the contrast between the black flint brickwork and the grey and white concrete cladding.[24]

A revised application for the development of the area on the summit of the hill was not presented for another two years and the buildings there, blighted by the long uncertainty, deteriorated further. Then, at the end of 1965, the city produced an application for four large eight-storey blocks standing baldly in the landscape, with a few low-rise houses and shops forlornly around the edge. The building contract had been negotiated, the planning application, submitted three weeks before the Christmas break, had on 3 January been stamped 'No objections raised', and the city council was about to grant itself planning permission when a local resident discovered what was afoot. He alerted neighbours, residents and amenity groups, sympathetic councillors and the press, who united in opposition to the proposals. Planning officers and members of the ruling party in the council were, however, determined to push their plans through, and it was only hours before the crucial council meeting when a telephone call from the Secretary of the Royal Fine Arts Commission finally persuaded the council to withdraw the scheme. The land was cleared but alternative plans were not drawn up for another two years.

At the same time as the city was producing designs for the public housing in Kingsdown, the Regional Health Authority was drawing up its plans for development of the 18 acres of land to the west, between St Michael's and Marlborough Hill. Though most of the proposed development was sited in the adjoining parish of St Michael's,[25] key parts of Kingsdown—more or less the lands once known as the Upper and Lower Montagues—were within the designated zone.

Objections to loss of homes in the area ran high. In particular the vicar of St Michael's, the Rev. Vyvyan Jones—with his parish threatened by the Hospital to the south-east, the new housing to the north-east and the University to the west—was active on behalf of his parishioners. A document produced by the hospital authorities in September 1969 states wryly, 'Acquisition of the majority of the 250 properties required for the first developments proved laborious and confirmed that, for major developments in a large town or city, action must be taken many years in advance of the planned project date.'

Outline plans for the site were published in July 1961 and work started in 1965/6 to the west of the King Edward VII building on the Bristol Royal Infirmary Queen's Building, followed by the monolithic 'Brutalist' blocks of Oncology (1967 start on site) and Maternity (1968 start on site).[26] It could have been even worse: thankfully neither the 14-storey ward block in the centre of the site, nor the three tower blocks of nurses' homes along Eugene Street, planned for the more distant future, were realised.

Over the coming years the Hospital Trust continued to acquire and demolish, or leave to decay, the remaining houses within the precinct. The slopes were covered by further unsightly additions, offices, stores and

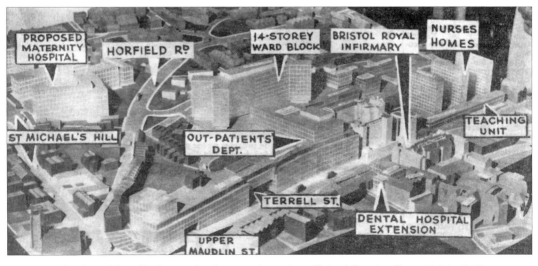

65   *Bristol Royal Infirmary development plans, 1961. (*Bristol Evening Post, *31 July 1961)*

workshops with *ad hoc* car parking on empty derelict sites. Kingsdown's skirmishes with the hospital authorities continued.

Only on the crest of the Down was a concentration of Georgian Kingsdown left, and for several years its existence, too, seemed threatened. The final details of Bristol's Development Plan were still to be resolved. The land west of Alfred Place, affecting 13 houses, was scheduled for a new primary school. The school roll at Kingsdown Secondary Modern School had fallen sharply as families moved out of the area and in 1963 it closed with only 93 pupils on the register.[27] A proposed link to the inner circuit road (planned in the late 1930s and running along Cotham Road just to the north of Kingsdown) was to run through Alfred Place. Kingsdown Parade and Somerset Street were to be a one-way circuit, Somerset Street being widened by compulsory purchase of the gardens to the north, and a new road linking 16c Kingsdown Parade and Somerset Street West End. The surviving early Georgian houses in the Upper Montagues were all within the hospital development zone. The triangle of land bounded by Kingsdown Parade, Clevedon Terrace and Horfield Road was earmarked for elderly persons' dwellings and the house on the site used by Bristol District Laundry to store its sheets was compulsorily purchased by the council—ostensibly to prevent industrial use on the site. Initially they planned to demolish the house, but when the Residents Association intervened, pointing out it was listed, they left it to decay. Parker's Bakery was replaced in 1964 by the industrial noise and fumes of Bollom the Dry Cleaners.

FIVE

The Late 20th and Early 21st Centuries

1970 to the present day: The Revival

Fortunately the late '60s saw a gradual growth in the popularity of inner-city living in Bristol, particularly among young and articulate professionals, and nowhere more so than in Kingsdown. As a lobbied member of the local Georgian Society wrote in 1971 in a letter to his national headquarters, 'Many of the new occupants [of Kingsdown] are architects, or university lecturers, or enlightened men of the law.' These new occupants were to prove a formidable partnership.

In 1971 the Kingsdown Conservation Group was formed, and in 1973 after several years of negotiation the area was formally designated a Conservation Area.[1] Over the following decades the group and individuals wrested Kingsdown back from its post-war dereliction. A local reporter in the early '70s put it well (if rather mixing his metaphors): 'There is a slight sense of siege about the remnants of Georgian Kingsdown; but the air is charged with that hopefulness which floods in to besieged people when relief is seen to be approaching in the distance. Like a man who has had an eye, a leg and an arm amputated, but still insists on getting around, Kingsdown refuses obstinately to die.'

It was to be a long but steady revival. Slowly the zoning lines drawn by post-war bureaucracy were more or less retracted. As the years went by, the non-residential uses that had taken advantage of Kingsdown's depressed years were encouraged to move. Residents defied their reluctant mortgage lenders and bought and restored the remaining fine Georgian houses. New houses were built on empty sites.

Following the city council's withdrawal of its plans for the summit of the Down, the houses and shops there lay derelict until the late '60s when most were demolished. Then, in 1967, the chastened city council decided to appoint independent architects.[2] Their brief was to return to the authority's original (1958) plans for the area and draw up a new scheme for low-rise high-density housing. By now the council had changed from Labour to Conservative control and it was

66   *High Kingsdown as built (*Bristol Evening Post, *21 July 1977).*

agreed, despite opposition from the Labour councillors, that the housing should be private rather than public.

High Kingsdown was completed between 1971 and 1974 and has proved very popular, winning both national and international prizes for its ground-breaking design. It is a compact pedestrian develop-ment, of similarly high density to the houses it replaced, with some one hundred two-storey patio houses set round small gardens, a linear six-storey block of 110 flats on the northern perimeter (originally designed as a buffer from the inner circuit road, then proposed for Cotham Road), together with a small supermarket and a children's playground.

In addition the city council built a new sports centre immediately to the east of the site. The Victorian Kingsdown Baths—'old and cold, though still fun and many children learnt to swim [there]' to quote a one-time resident—had been pulled down in the early '70s, with the understanding that the council would incorporate a new pool in the redevelopment proposals. But then, despite many residents' protests, it was not included in the final designs—'cut for reasons of cost … to be in Phase 2'. The new centre, without a pool, was opened in 1975 and is well used. There has been no Phase 2 though.

The High Kingsdown flats included provision for 40 elderly persons, and Housing Association wardened flats were built at the same time on the site of the redundant Portland Chapel in Portland Street. As a result, the local authority judged that the planned elderly persons' dwellings at the end of the Parade were no longer needed. The land once occupied by Bristol District Laundry, which the council had bought in anticipation, was sold as surplus to requirements in 1972, enabling the site to return to residential use.

Plans for the proposed primary school on the land between Alfred Place and Kingsdown School were not dropped until the early 1980s when, with falling birth rates and two other primary schools nearby, the county council finally decided that a further school was no longer needed. In 1982 the site at the west end of Alfred Place was sold and developed as a terrace of private houses,[3] although the anomaly of the 1935 Road Improvement Line, linked in the 1950s to the building of the school, remained on the books for several more years.

It took until nearly the end of the century to return Parker's Bakery site on Kingsdown Parade from light industrial use to residential. Bollom's moved out in 1966, residents having successfully fought as far as a public inquiry an application to install a 95ft chimney, forced on the firm by the new Clean Air laws. An application was then lodged on behalf of the East London Kray brothers to turn the site into a nightclub. Again the residents protested. Peter Nicholls, the playwright, then living immediately behind the site in St Matthews Road, wrote to the council, 'As our bedroom will be a mere 20 feet from the rear of the warehouse, it seems to me we will have no alternative but to offer our private lives as a cabaret entertainment, or sell up and leave.' Permission was refused, but instead there was further industrial use and expansion of the site by four more houses, to form two warehouses.

It was to take another 25 years for the land to revert to housing, and over that time Kingsdown suffered from the increasingly larger trucks of the wholesale firms—an electrical factor, a shipping agent, a coin-operated gaming machines distributor—who occupied the site during these decades. During the '70s all but one of the firms left for more suitable premises on the edge of the city, closer to the newly built motorway. Bristol Coin Equipment (BCE) remained until 1993, though, distributing their gaming machines throughout Bristol.

By the 1990s Kingsdown was again seen as a desirable residential area and the director of BCE decided to realise his assets. Kingsdown residents' initial joy soon turned to apprehension. The first overly dense scheme was for 120 flats on a site where historically there had been 10 houses. They were to be occupied by Bristol University students and a large L-shaped four-storey hostel-type building was to run along the Back of Kingsdown Parade and up Clevedon Terrace. After lobbying by residents the scheme was withdrawn. Eight months later a revised application was presented, a scheme of 41 two-bedroom flats. With many years of experience, residents were now expert objectors, and this scheme was refused by the planners as both too dense and lacking an appropriate residential mix.

A further four schemes were presented and refused, but in July 1994 permission was finally granted. To the relief of residents the final scheme, though by no means perfect, was for a mix of seven houses and 23 flats.

The saga, however, was not over. It turned out that the owner of BCE did not own the entire site. 'Kings Mews' to the east was constructed more or less according to the July plans, but then all went quiet for three years. Finally, in May 1997, a new application was lodged for the western half. Different architects were used and it was a very different scheme from that of three years earlier: eight three- and four-storey terraced houses and a detached house at the junction of Clevedon Terrace and Kingsdown Parade.[4] Again the residents responded, and the detached house was removed and building heights lowered.

At last the site of 35-51 Kingsdown Parade, in industrial use for over sixty years, was totally residential once more.

The heavy goods vehicles of the warehouses were not the only traffic problem threatening Kingsdown in those decades. With the opening of the M32 in the early 1970s, Kingsdown found itself part of a 'rat run' between the motorway and western Bristol. By the early 1980s some five hundred vehicles an hour were counted going through Fremantle Square in the rush hour.

The Conservation Group met with Avon highway engineers and organised the first public meeting at a packed and emotional event in King Square in 1983. However, plans involving road-closures, one-way systems and 'no entries' were still under discussion more than six years later. Neighbouring amenity societies were concerned that traffic would be diverted onto their streets instead, and some residents that they would find Kingsdown almost impossible to get out of. Then an eight-year-old resident of Kingsdown Parade was knocked down and seriously injured crossing the road by his home and the matter was at last seen by the authorities to be urgent. In 1991/2 the road scheme, more or less that still in place today, was finally implemented with a significant reduction in through traffic.

From its founding in 1971 the Kingsdown Conservation Group fought, with mixed success, for the redrawing of the hospital precinct boundary at the north-west corner of Kingsdown and the protection and release of the Georgian houses in it. In 1977 the Health Authority released three areas within the precinct: the part of Kingsdown lying east of Marlborough Hill and north of Marlborough Hill Place; and two areas on St Michaels Hill. A fourth area west of Marlborough Hill, which included some of the oldest houses in Kingsdown, they refused to relinquish.

However, the tireless work of the group in lobbying the council and others was beginning to pay off and official attitudes towards wholesale redevelopment were slowly changing. In 1979, the Health

Authority, having previously purchased and demolished other houses in the precinct,[5] submitted an application to knock down Blenheim House just below the summit of Marlborough Hill.[6] They had bought it in 1968, only to leave it empty and increasingly derelict for the next 13 years despite pressure from the Conservation Group and others and its Spot Listing by the Department of the Environment. To the Health Authority's annoyance, permission to demolish was refused by the city planners. Two years later they sold the house to a local architect, who lovingly restored it for his own use. Later still, they agreed to remove it and its immediate neighbours from the precinct.

In 1984 the Hospital Trust's ten-year plans for further major expansion of the Bristol Royal Infirmary on the precinct site began to emerge.

67 *Bristol Royal Infirmary development plans, 1986. A: proposed extension to the maternity hospital; B: proposed ward development; C/E: alternative sites for new car parks; D: future wards.*

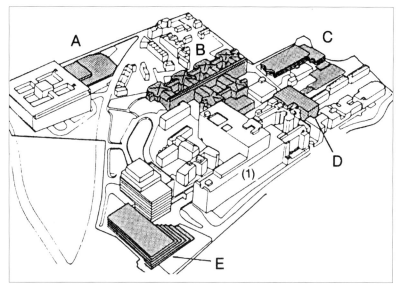

68 *Cartoon by Mark Vyvyan Jones in response to suggestion of a new car park immediately opposite Marlborough Hill Place.* (Bristol Evening Post, *9 July 1986)*

After two years of informal discussions with the local councils and the Conservation Group, the Health Authority's architect presented the proposed scheme to the public. It included 250 new beds in a long five-storey block built over the road known as Cottage Place (halfway down Marlborough Hill to the west) and a multi-storey car park for 300 cars immediately opposite the Georgian houses on Marlborough Hill Place. The Health Authority's architect was quoted in the *Evening Post* as saying: 'We have been completely open with everything, but we do disagree with most of what Kingsdown Conservation Group says.'[7]

The group had protested that, besides blighting the adjacent houses in Kingsdown, the plans were poorly thought out and aggravated rather than improved an already tortuous hospital site layout that had difficult access, a poor working environment and complicated internal arrangements. They proposed that any development should be lower down the site, closer to existing entrances and bus routes. Two architect members of the Conservation Group produced alternative plans illustrating that the same quantity of development could be provided in accordance with these principles, which they presented to the Hospital Board. They also suggested that the hospital should carry out a masterplan study to guide future development and ensure that only those facilities that needed a central site would be located there.

After deliberation the hospital withdrew its application and retired to take a more holistic view of the site and reconsider its options. The possibility of removing the main hospital to a green field site was even included in the ideas discussed.[8] Such a radical step was not taken, but when in 2006 new plans were presented for the site on the slope, some of the lessons of the previous twenty years had been learnt by the authority. The main development in Kingsdown, a new Heart Centre, was sited below Cottage Place and multi-storey car parks were no longer on the agenda.

Recent decades have seen the gradual repair and infill of Kingsdown's urban fabric. Most of the surviving Georgian houses have been restored to their former glory and gap sites have been filled. The bottoms of many of the long gardens have been developed with small terraced houses on the north sides of Somerset Street and Dove Street, although local pressure on the council stopped new development of this sort in Somerset Street in 1978, a ban reinforced in 2008.

In 2000 the bomb site of no. 10 Kingsdown Parade (where since the war two one-storey prefabs had housed a day centre for Social Services) came up for sale and provided an opportunity for residents to influence development more directly. Conscious of how easy it would be to destroy Kingsdown's 18th-century heritage with unsympathetic and over-dense development of this important site, a hundred residents formed a co-operative to buy the land from the council and develop the site. Their aim was to produce a scheme that would be a suitable 21st-century contribution to the area, with any profits being used for environmental projects that would benefit the community. A limited architectural competition was held, the resulting drawings were displayed in the prefabs for people to express their preference, and finally an architect was chosen.[9]

It was the first co-operative redevelopment project of its kind in the city, and though the city council was very sympathetic and prepared to wait for its money the residents found, like those Georgian developers two centuries before, that there were a number of financial and legal hurdles to overcome. The project manager, a long-time resident architect, had a difficult role. It was not an easy site to develop, unknown cellars were discovered, builders were difficult and purchasers, many of them already resident in Kingsdown, demanding. Finally though, in 2004, seven houses, two maisonettes and a flat were completed in a style considered sympathetic to the Georgian context, but very much of its time. The scheme had successfully achieved its major goals. All the original investors got their money back but, perhaps unsurprisingly, there were no profits for community projects.

The years of fighting the various authorities have no doubt been a factor in forging a strong and vibrant community in Kingsdown, and over the past 35 years the 'new' residents have enjoyed celebrating their fellowship. In 1973, to mark the declaration of the Conservation Area, they held the

69 *Kingsdown Parade, west end, built on the site of no. 10.*

70   *Kingsdown Street Fair, 1980s.*

first modern street fair in Bristol since the closing of St James's Fair in Victorian times, and in 1987 they celebrated the quarter of a millennium since that first scheme on the King's Down was drawn up, in a whole year of activities called 'Kingsdown 250'.

That first street fair was initially seen as a one-off party, but its success meant it soon became an annual event. The early fairs held in Kingsdown Parade were very urban affairs, with the street closed to traffic and filled with stalls, activities and entertainment, which attracted people from all over Bristol. Residents manned and patronised stalls, played music and bought bric-a-brac at auction. The children bounced on inflatables, whacked the rat and had their faces painted. There were cream teas in gardens, roundabouts on parking spaces and morris dancing at the crossroads. Every year large sums were raised for charity.

Later, with fears that it had become too popular and that older residents felt threatened, it became smaller, mainly for residents and their friends. Recently it has had a strong ecological bias, the wide range of activities including competitions for homegrown produce and the best homemade preserves. It provides an opportunity for residents to meet and renew the sense of community that is so integral a part of living in Kingsdown.

In November 1985, encouraged by their experience of running successful street fairs, a group of some twenty Kingsdown residents met in the sitting room of a house in Kingsdown Parade and agreed they should celebrate the quarter of a millennium since Tully's first plans for the slopes of the Down in 1737. The flow of ideas included an exhibition, music, drama, guided walks, a community party, a 'special' street fair, involvement of local schools and a church service. Kingsdown's history, as we have seen, has been entwined with that of Bristol, and the residents were keen that Kingsdown's celebration should be a Bristol event as well as a Kingsdown one.

In the event Kingsdown did it all. That first meeting had envisaged activities spreading over a few weeks, two months at the most, but the

71 '*Kingsdown 250*' *exhibition at the City Museum, 1987. The most striking exhibit in the Georgian section was a life-size model of Patrick Cotter (1760-1806), known as 'Patrick O'Brien The Irish Giant'. At 8ft 1in he was, according to the* Guinness Book of Records, *the seventh tallest man in the world ever—and the owner, though not himself a resident, of two houses in Kingsdown Parade.*

Brought over to Bristol from Ireland in 1779, Cotter's first appearance was at St James's Fair. Later he travelled the length and breadth of the country displaying his gigantic self to crowds at fairs or in private rooms. The Georgians loved such spectacles, and he was extremely successful. In Bristol in 1780 he is recorded as earning £30 in three days—over £3,000 in today's money. The giant invested his earnings in property, including the two Kingsdown houses which are long since demolished and part of the site of Kings Mews.

activities lasted for ten months, with regular pre-event social gatherings in the preceding year keeping local people informed and involved.

The museum exhibition took the visitor through the events of 250 years with a series of defined spaces. On one wall were panels telling Kingsdown's story, while authentic materials and artefacts were displayed in ambitious room settings from the relevant period, constructed by local residents. The Georgian section had an elegant panelled drawing room, with pedimented door and dado rail—all materials from Kingsdown, some salvaged from skips at the time of demolition—and a life-size model of the Irish Giant opposite a *trompe-l'oeil* garden wall. The Victorian section had heavily patterned wallpaper found in a resident's attic as background to photographic portraits of Victorian residents, a cast-iron fireplace and an upright piano. The 20th-century 'Under Threat' section showed stark and evocative monochrome photographs of local buildings lost or threatened during the post-war development of the area. The 20th-century 'Today' section had a specially commissioned collection of colour photographs of Kingsdown in all its 1987 glory.

The exhibition was followed by two concerts, one in St Michael's Church with a programme of baroque music and a candle-lit performance of 18th-century music in St George's Brandon Hill given by a group of musicians in costume, which was interspersed with readings about Bristol and Kingsdown.

Meanwhile teachers in the two local primary schools incorporated the story of Kingsdown into their lessons. Children learnt about the history of the area, interviewed elderly local residents, and walked around the area observing architectural details. All was recorded in an impressive display of artwork on classroom walls.

At the end of May there was a community play. The initial idea of dramatising events in Kingsdown history had been floated rather cautiously, but a local writer showed interest in staging a community play and offered to bring in other professionals to help. A venue was found—the original 11th-century parish church of St James. Since 1984 it had been closed and empty so, besides providing a

72 *Kingsdown community play* The Nine Trees' Shade, *1987, held in St James Priory Church (Bristol News and Media)*

most appropriate location, this was an opportunity to draw attention to its plight and possibly stimulate interest in finding a future use for it.[10] Regular drama workshops were held where over 200 people, from Kingsdown and surrounding areas, of varying ages and experience, gradually wove themselves into a coherent whole. The number of speaking parts had to be expanded from 40 to 80 to meet the talents and enthusiasm of the actors, while some parts were double cast, to ensure that no one felt excluded. Non-actors made costumes and sets and converted the church into an auditorium suitable for a promenade performance.

The Nine Trees' Shade—a reference to the row of elm trees that once stood at the top of Nine Tree Hill—was set in 1737 with the action revolving round St James's Fair. The churchyard was transformed into a fairground with stalls, freak shows and lively music. Inside, the sanctuary became a large proscenium stage, while walkways over the pews led to smaller stages providing settings for fairground booths, sideshows and a hospital ward. The audience were encouraged to promenade during the performance, becoming spectators both in and out of the play.

By the middle of October all the suggestions at that first meeting had been realised. The museum staff said the exhibition had been one of the most popular shows they had ever had. The play had played to packed audiences over seven nights and was hailed as a triumph for community theatre and for Kingsdown. The concerts and the involvement of local schools and churches had exceeded all expectations, the street fair had been a visual delight with many of the residents and stallholders decked out in their play costumes, and the two guided walks around the area had proved so popular that an extra guide had to be organised.

1737 had been well commemorated and for a long time Kingsdown residents glowed with contented pride. What had been a celebration of Kingsdown history had become part of that history.

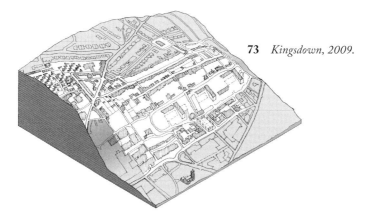

73   *Kingsdown, 2009.*

The Present Day

Though one can never relax in the inner city, Kingsdown in the early 21st century can hopefully look forward to a more secure future. Many of the houses on the summit continue to be occupied by architects, academics and the legal profession, along with a varied mix of other occupations. A few of those original pioneers of the 1960s and '70s are still there, rather more grey perhaps but still very involved. Now, as then, several of the larger houses in Kingsdown Parade are let to students, though increasing numbers have returned to single-family use over the years.

To the south-east, the flats continue to feel out of place, but they answer an ever-present need for social housing. They remain popular because of their central location and undoubtedly provide residents with outstanding views over Bristol.

To the north-west, High Kingsdown remains a popular example of successful post-war urban housing. Though a bid in 2002 for it to become a Conservation Area was refused by English Heritage, the inspector commented that 'when more research has been completed on this building type, the decision should be re-assessed ... we are only just beginning to understand [the architecture of the early 1970s].'

Buying a house on Kingsdown's summit is no longer the bargain it was in the 1960s, '70s and earlier, but thanks to dual incomes and the variety of house types and sizes, families with young children—essential residents for any vibrant community—somehow manage to afford to buy homes. Regular communal events continue to be organised.

Despite the vicissitudes of history, the residents of Kingsdown—to misquote the 1765 poet—can still happily say:

> Oh lovely Kingsdown! Nature's sweet Parade!
> Our delight at Morn and Even Tide,
> To breathe thy healthy Air, and view thy prospects wide ...

Appendix

The Dighton family

The various Dighton family transactions relating to the Kingsdown fields that can be dated with certainty are:

The Montagues

1666 John Teague, leather seller, and William Davis, merchant, sold to Henry Dighton and his heirs two closes of land called Montague.

1677 Henry's widow, Katherine, gave the land in trust to her four daughters, Mary, Martha, Catherine and Sarah.

1691 After Katherine's death a chirograph of a fine (a legal device which put an end to any controversy about land ownership) established the lawful ownership of the Montagues by Mary m. to John Foot, Martha m. to Thos. Hicks, Katherine m. to Robert Bound and Sarah m. to John Jones.

1730 Sarah had died leaving her quarter share to Henry Foot, her nephew. Another fine established the ownership of the 18 acres, *viz.* Henry Foot ½, Robert Bound ¼, Samuel Merrick (related by marriage) and others, trustees for Martha Hicks, ¼.

Prior Hill and Pigeon House Close

1701 George Dighton, eldest son of Henry Dighton, bequeathed the two closes to his wife, Judith, and thence to their eldest son, Isaac. Judith bequeathed Pigeon House Close and the ground called Little Prior Hill to their second son, William. Isaac and William died without issue while Judith was still living and on her death the estate descended to their five daughters, Mary m. Christopher Scandrett, Ann m. Geo. Bearpacker, Judith m. – Hughes, Elizabeth m. – Lowe and Martha m. Wm. Dighton, as co-heirs.

1737 The daughters, or their descendents, conveyed the property in trust to Mary's son John Scandrett, Elizabeth's son-in-law Oliver Jelfe, and others.

The Dighton family were active participants in the life of St James's parish and several are commemorated in memorial tablets in St James's Church. Henry, and his sons and grandsons, served variously as members of the vestry, churchwardens and overseers of the poor, and they and their wives made bequests to the parish in their wills. Henry gave an annuity to buy coats for 10 poor men of the parish forever and his wife left money for the benefit of 10 poor widows. Later their daughter Katherine Bound, in her will dated 1702, wished her legacy to be used to buy apparel for eight poor women. She qualified her bequest by stipulating that the money first be paid 'to my poor relations, if any need it'. However, her great-nephew, adjudicating in 1736, stated that their only needy relation had been dead for four years, so 'I think it incumbent on the Overseers of the Poor of the parish of St James to see that the poor of the parish are not wronged of this gift and that the same be put up in the Table of the Church to prevent Smothering of the same for the Future.' (PRO 99/31g) All these legacies were to be charged on the profits arising from the Kingsdown lands.

The Dighton Succession

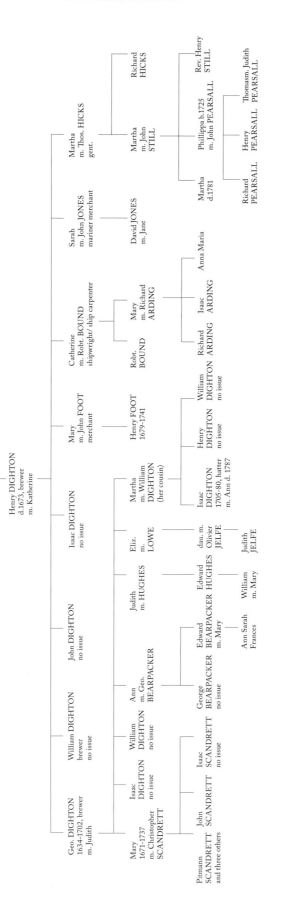

Notes

ONE *The King's Down*

1. M.W. Ponsford, *Excavations at Grey Friars, Bristol*, 1975.
2. Wm. Barrett, *The History and Antiquities of the City of Bristol*, 1789, reprint 1982, p.29.
3. Ponsford, *op. cit.* and correspondence with the author.
4. Variously Marshal or Marshall. To Marshal—to arrange or draw up (soldiers) in order for fighting, exercise or review (S.O.D.).
5. William of Worcestre, *The Topography of Medieval Bristol*, sect. 192, ed. and trans. Frances Neale, 2000.
6. W. Dugdale, *A history of the Abbeys*, etc., 1823.
7. Later Priory buildings extended from the gatehouse in Lewins Mead to the eastern end of the Barton, with additional buildings in what is now Broadmead.
8. BRO/P/StJ/ChW/6.
9. Certificate of the Commissioners, Dispensations Act 1536.
10. BRO P/StJ/D/8/1, just under £200,000 in today's money.
11. A deed relating to the partition of St James, Bristol. See proceedings of the Clifton Antiquarian Club, 1899, pp.109-38.
12. De Gomme, 'The Siege and Capture of Bristol by the Royalist Forces in 1643', *Journal of Army Historical Research*, eds. C. Firth and J.H. Leslie, vol. 4, no. 15.
13. John Lynch, *For King and Parliament: Bristol and the Civil War*, p.37.
14. Russell James, *The Civil War Defences of Bristol*, p.25.
15. J.F. Nicholls and John Taylor, *Bristol Past and Present*, vol. I, p.299.
16. Richard Atkyns, *Military Memoirs of the Civil War*, ed. Peter Young, 1967.
17. Joshua Sprigge, *Anglia Rediviva*, 1854.
18. Thomas Rainsborough, *A true relation of the storming of Bristol*, 1645.
19. Oliver Cromwell, Letter to the Speaker of the House of Commons.
20. Sprigge, *op. cit.*
21. Nicholls and Taylor, *op. cit.*, vol. III, p.10.
22. Sprigge, *op. cit.*
23. John Latimer, *The Annals of Bristol in the 17th century*, p.193.
24. Samuel Seyer, *Memoirs historical and topographical of Bristol and its neighbours*, vol. II.
25. *Ibid.*, p.305.
26. BRO 03457 (1-35).
27. P/StJ/D/6.

TWO *From the King's Down to Kingsdown*

1. Daniel Defoe, *A Journey through Britain*, 1724.
2. St James Square, now demolished, was sited just to the east of where St James Barton

roundabout is now. It was part blitzed, part cleared for post-war development.

3. Previously known as Upper Bull Lane.

4. *Felix Farley's Bristol Journal*, December 1760.

5. Dr R.H. Leech, *An Archaeological Desk Evaluation of no. 6 Kingsdown Parade and adjacent properties*, 1998.

6. Rocque's map shows only a single house and garden on the site, but it would seem that there were actually two houses there, for those 1740 sales deeds refer to 'that messuage … built by said Giles Greville [and] a messuage built by said Ralph Good lately erected'. Documents also show that Greville had previously caused Good much anxiety about the effects of structural and drainage problems on his house. The former's landscaping works, raising the ground considerably higher than it had been formerly, was hardly conducive to the peace and tranquillity expected of a summer house.

7. The stable had been converted into a house by 1760. The small house on the site today, though on the original foundations, is of the 20th century.

8. No. 6 Kingsdown Parade and nos 15 and 17 Marlborough Hill. Nos 4 Kingsdown Parade and 15 Marlborough Hill and the houses further down the slope were all demolished in the 20th century.

9. The houses are shown at the front of their sites, when in practice all the original buildings are at the rear. The houses now fronting Kingsdown Parade at that point are all later additions, in the gardens.

10. No. 7 Kingsdown Parade, demolished 1960s.

11. Now confusingly known as 28 St Matthew's Road.

12. Nos 26 and 25 St Matthew's Road. For the romantics, no. 26, or Portway House, has the possibility of a tunnel entrance: a door in the lowest and southernmost end of the large vaulted cellars below the house. Certainly the house has a suggestive name. There is also a good story told locally of the daughters of the Boyce family, the owners of the house for the first half of the 20th century. The young Misses Boyce, on their own one night, heard a noise in the cellar. On going down to investigate, they found an extremely drunk sailor, who explained to the credulous girls that he had wandered some hours previously into wine vaults down in the city and to his bewilderment had ended up in Portway House. The two children, believing his story, let him out the front door—doubtless to the great relief of the quick-witted burglar. Many years later Esme, still a firm believer in the tunnel's existence, recalled that the cellars had appeared to have stalls in them, which she had always presumed were used to house the donkeys which went along the secret passageway. The two sons of the house apparently tried to explore the cellar further, but their activities caused a landfall and their father forbade further investigation. Later owners of Portway House are more sceptical, and an expert consulted at Bristol Museum commented that he had no specific knowledge of this Kingsdown example, but his department had investigated similar 'entrances' elsewhere in Bristol and found they led merely to another vaulted wine cellar, or subterranean cool store. In no case had he found any tunnel leading off.

13. No. 6 Kingsdown Parade, although it seems the house we see today was not the first on the site. Roger Leech has found a single-room cellar, slightly offset to the house, which he thinks was that of the original garden house. The current house, he surmises, is late 18th- or even early 19th-century.

14. Nos 13, 17 (Blenheim House) and 19 Marlborough Hill.

15. Demolished 1942.

16. *Felix Farley's Bristol Journal*, December 1760.

17. The city was to concede the position of England's main slavery port to Liverpool a decade later.

18. *Felix Farley's Bristol Journal*, 1765.

19. Kingsdown Mead along the summit was not included in the Tully Plan.

20. Probably Judith and Oliver Jelfe, George Bearpacker, Pitman Scandrett, Isaac Scandrett, Isaac and Martha Dighton and William Hughes.

21. George Tully, d. 1770, who later owned two houses in King Square, one for his own residence, one for letting (W. Ison, *The Georgian Buildings of Bristol*, p.174).

22. King Square was initially known as New Square. The limes were removed in 1838 (Stewart Harding and David Lambert, *Parks and Gardens of Avon*, 1994) to be replaced by a border of shrubs and trees surrounded by 'a light and elegant iron palisade'. The railings were removed during the Second World War and the arched lamp holders soon after, but these were restored by Bristol City Council in 1994.

23. Gay Street, running between Duke Street and Dove Street, and much of Hillgrove Street were demolished by Bristol City Council in the 1960s. Spring Hill was initially known as Square Lane.

24. A.H. Gomme, M. Jenner and Bryan D.G. Little, *An Architectural History of Bristol*.

25. Nos 57 and 59 Kingsdown Parade, for example.

26. Bristol's first bank opened in March 1750.

27. Ison, *op. cit.*, p.175.

28. *Felix Farley's Bristol Journal*, 13 December 1760.

29. Ashmead's map of 1828 and the 1885 O.S. map.

30. George Bearpacker and Isaac Dighton.

31. Sketchley's Bristol Directory 1775 gives an alphabetical list of Bristol's merchants and tradesmen. Some private residents had their names included, but not all, which means it is a close, but not necessarily comprehensive, record of early residents in Kingsdown.

32. Deeds of no. 15 Somerset Street

33. Demolished *c.*1886, now the site of nos 37-40 Somerset Street: deeds of 41 Somerset Street.

34. 1885 sales advertisement. No. 12 Kingsdown Parade also had a 'large turret or observatory' on the roof, but how common these were, or indeed whether they were for astronomical observation or for enjoying the extensive Kingsdown view, is still to be discovered.

35. Kingsdown Parade is referred to in 1738 deeds as 'a way or road leading from a close called Kings Down to a certain road or way formerly called Horfield Lane'; 'Kingsdown Street' in deeds of the 1750s and '60s; 'the Parade, King's down' in the 1775 Directory; and only in the 1785 directory is there mention of the name Kingsdown Parade. To confuse further, the houses fronting directly onto the north side of the Parade from Horfield Road to Clevedon Terrace were originally known as Montague Parade; and the houses at the east end variously as James's Place, St James Place and St James Parade. Even early census and directory takers were unclear: the 1841 census heads a page 'St James Place', but then lists residents that the Directory gives as living in Kingsdown Parade. Not until the rationalisation of all Bristol street names from the 1860s was the street naming, together with the house numbering, finally resolved.

36. John Latimer, *Annals of Bristol*, vol. 2, p. 404.

37. Bryan Little, 'Georgian Bristol: the future of 18th-century Kingsdown', *Gloucester Countryside*, 1957.

38. The Rev. Vyvyan Jones, vicar of St Michael's Church, fighting its demolition.

39. An early resident was the poet Samuel Taylor Coleridge (1772-1834), who lived briefly in Oxford Street in 1796. Forty years later, from 1834-6, the Rev. George Muller (1805-98), founder of the Muller Homes for Orphans, was at no. 21 Paul Street (both houses are now demolished).

40. *Felix Farley's Bristol Journal*, 1765.

41. Anything other than minimal identification is difficult. Until the late 1770s the various tax returns listed all the Kingsdown residents together under 'Eugene Street' or 'Upper Montagues', and only later 'Eugene Street and Kingsdown' (in tiny letters). The task of parish rate collecting was not a popular one and the records of St James have copious, often barely literate, letters from men, or their wives, begging to be excused their turn of being abused: a return of 1771 listing 'all the men householders'

in Kingsdown has the addition after one Thomas Hammond's name, 'he said on paying you may all kiss his backside'!

42. Latimer, *op. cit.*, vol. 2, p.318.

43. Destroyed in the Second World War.

44. Several members of the Ash family lived in Kingsdown: Edward lived at no. 18 until 1810, before moving to 86 Kingsdown Parade, where he lived until his death in 1818. His oldest son, Gregory, lived next door at no. 19 from 1796 until his death in 1819 and his younger son, Richard, lived in Ashley House, 14 Somerset Street between 1813 and 1819, before moving to Cotham House.

45. For a full account see Ronald Mayo, *The Huguenots in Bristol*, 1985.

46. George Oliver, *Collections Illustrating the History of the Catholic Religion in the Counties of Cornwall, Devon, Dorset, Somerset, Wiltshire and Gloucester.*

47. Bishop Secker's Diocese Book.

48 Oliver, *op. cit.*, p.108.

49 On his visits to Bristol John Wesley would often stay at no. 6 Dighton Street, the home of John Castelman, surgeon. In September 1784 he notes in his diary how, when staying at this house, he 'took a step which I had long weighed in my mind and appointed Mr. Whatcoat and Mr. Vasey to go and serve the desolate sheep in America'.

50. I am indebted to R.J.H. Burgess, author of an unpublished family history, for much information on the Lucas family.

51. No. 12 Kingsdown Parade.

52. David Richardson, *Bristol, Africa and the Eighteenth-Century Slave Trade to America*, vol. 3, 1991, p.110.

53. Richardson, *op. cit.*, vol. 3, p.109.

54. *Ibid.*, vol. 4, 1996, p.70.

55. Mathews, *Bristol Directory* 1793-4, pp.38-9.

56. Richardson, *op. cit.*, vol. 4, p.188. The *Lioness* on this 1791/2 trip is described in the returns as a wood ship (i.e. not a slave ship).

57. Robert Lucas's house is a good example of the difficulties facing the architectural historian. In the 1780s his son-in-law, James Lockier, who had bought no. 12 from Lucas's son, 'improved and enlarged on the north-westward part of ... [the] plot', doubling the house in size and remaking the Parade elevation to render the enlargement seamless on the front, as it is today. The south-facing elevation, on the other hand, remains as two conjoined houses very different in appearance. Following James Lockier's bankruptcy in 1793 the house was sold, but continued to be lived in as a family house by the vendors. Then, a hundred years and two owners later, in 1878, the house was bought by a firm of builders, who set out over the next few years to maximise their profits on the site: the main house was 'divided by them into two messuages or dwelling houses', forming today's nos 12 and 12a; and in the 1880s three houses,12b-d, were built where the stable block/coach house and side garden had been. In the 1970s the house was further divided by the conversion of the top garret floor of both houses into a single penthouse flat. In today's numbering the Lucas house is no. 12 and the extended part of the house no.12a. The house built by James Lockier which features in the advertisement, no. 10, was destroyed in the Second World War.

58. See P. Mellor, *A Kingsdown Community*, 1985 for a detailed description of the development of St James Place.

59. Latimer, *op. cit.*, vol. 2, p.494.

60. Nos 73 and 75 Kingsdown Parade.

61. Nos 23, 24 and 25 Somerset Street.

62. Following the closure of the Chapel in 1970, the Knightstone Housing wardened flats were built on the site.

63. No. 3 Portland Street.

64. A.J. Lambert, *The Chapel on the Hill*, 1929.
65. The whole site for no. 34 and Devon House (34a) in Kingsdown Parade had been sold for development some fifty years previously in 1766 but was only split in 1816 when the garden was purchased by a William Reed, who built a good and substantial house.
66. John Evans, *A Chronological Outline of the History of Bristol*, p.202.
67. *Bristol Mirror*, 10 November 1838.
68. *Ibid.*, 9 November 1822; *Bristol Mercury*, 11 November 1822.
69. *Bristol Mercury*, 12 November 1836.
70. No. 21 Kingsdown Parade.
71. No. 65 Kingsdown Parade.
72. *Bristol Mirror*, 9 November 1822, 10 November 1838; *Bristol Mercury*, 11 November 1822, 7 November 1835, 12 November 1835, 12 November 1836, 10 November 1838, 9 November 1839.
73. *Bristol Mirror*, 10 November 1838.
74. *Bristol Times*, 7 November 1867.
75. A dinner bill sent by the landlord of the *Montague* to the *Bristol Times* and *Bristol Mirror* in 1873. John Latimer, *op. cit.*, vol. 3, p.78.
76. BRO 6098(26).
77. Possibly, from its position on the map, Giles Greville's original summer house.
78. Landscape contractors pruning one of the trees on the site a few years back were alarmed to find their saw suddenly hitting shrapnel embedded in a large branch.
79. The remaining houses on Montague Green were demolished by Bristol following a Clearance Order in 1958.

THREE   *From Suburb to Inner City*

1. Is it significant, or just coincidence, that sometime in the puritanical 17th century Whorestone Close was renamed Steep Hill and, on the other side of St Michael's Hill, Fockynggrove became Puckingrove?
2. A short distance away, near the site of the Stokes Croft sallyport, another skeleton—believed to be that of a Royalist defender clubbed by the butt of a musket and buried where he fell—was found when Jamaica Street was extended in 1872 (*Bristol Times and Bristol Mirror*, July 1872). And, more recently still, the current owners of a house at the west end of Kingsdown found a large cannon ball buried in their garden.
3. W.J. Jackson, *The Story of Kingsdown, Bristol Times and Bristol Mirror*, 23 November 1909.
4. *Ibid.*
5. James Russell, *The Civil War Defences of Bristol*, p.26.
6. Nos 41-2 Somerset Street, originally known as North Somerset Street but renumbered and renamed when the Observatory House site was developed in *c.*1885.
7. Many Georgian house deeds are very specific about banning antisocial activities on the part of the residents. Deeds for no. 20 in Somerset Street for instance specify that there should be 'no turpentine work, sulphur work, vitriol work, colour work, lead work, glass work, soap work, smelting house, or the trades or businesses of a soap boiler, chandler, brewer, distiller, maltster, brazier, founder, coppersmith, black or white smith, farrier, butcher, catgut maker, currier, or any lime brick or pipe kiln, slaughterhouse, or any other business that would be a nuisance or offensive to persons residing thereabouts.'
8. The Pugsleys' burial place was marked, at some unknown date, by a monumental tablet on the boundary wall of Observatory House, close to the site of the fort. The exact place of burial has been identified as the boundary between numbers 40 and 41, but the plaque disappeared, it seems, during demolition (Russell James, *The Civil War Defences of Bristol*, p.26).
9. John Evans, *A Chronological Outline of the History of Bristol*, p.202.

10. P/StJ/OP/1/1-20 Parish Rate books.
11. J. Charlton and P.M. Milton, *Redland 791-1800*, 1951. A 'wald' is OE: a wood, a forest.
12. A deed relating to the partition of property in St James's, Bristol. See Proceedings of the Clifton Antiquarian Club, 1898.
13. Anon., *Bristol Curiosities*, 1854.
14. The garden wall is between 10 Nugent Hill and 2 Clare Road, the wellhead at the end of no. 2's garden.
15. H.O. Wills II and III lived in Ashley House, 14 Somerset Street: H.O. Wills II, the second son of the tobacco firm's founder, from 1837 until 1860 and his son H.O. Wills III until 1863.
16. Sue Hardiman, *The 1832 Cholera Epidemic and its impact on the City of Bristol*, 2005.
17. Latimer, *op. cit.*, vol. 3, 1887.
18. *Health of Towns Commission Report on the State of Bristol*, HMSO, 1845.
19. Water closets were first patented in 1775 and generally available from 1787. Some of the Kingsdown houses of the late Georgian period would probably have had them as a standard fitting: the 1794 advertisement for 10 Kingsdown Parade mentions one on the first floor, but detailed specifications of St James Place make no mention of their provision.
20. Deeds for no. 12 Somerset Street.
21. Nos 22-8 Kingsdown Parade.
22. Deeds of 24 Kingsdown Parade.
23. Spring Hill Villa. Its near neighbour, 20 Somerset Street, had a 'cistern or reservoir' under its kitchen that was shared with its immediate neighbour. The cistern was divided in two, each house pumping up its own rainwater, but if the water rose over the dividing wall, then it was agreed the surplus could be used by both houses.
24. Latimer, *op. cit.*, vol. 3, p.312, 1887.
25. David Large and Frances Round, *Public Health in Mid-Victorian Bristol*, 1974, p.6.
26. *Ibid.*, pp.1-9.
27. Ash could be sold on by the scavengers to be used in the manufacture of (low quality) bricks or mortar.
28. Harold Nabb, *The Bristol Gas Industry 1815-1949*, 1987.
29. Latimer, *Annals of Bristol in the 19th century*, 1887, pp.43-4.
30. *Ibid.*, vol. 3, p.230.
31. William Sturge (1820-1905) lived at 25 Somerset Street.
32. Elizabeth Sturge, *Reminiscences of My Life*.
33. No. 52 Kingsdown Parade.
34. Observatory House, Somerset Street.
35. *Bristol Times*, 22 January 1842.
36. No. 1 King Square.
37. *Bristol Times*, 2 January 1875.
38. As in 12b-d Kingsdown Parade built on the site of the stables of no. 12a.
39. As in 30-3 Montague Hill built in the garden of Dundry House (20 Kingsdown Parade).
40. Sometimes called Somerset House, as was later, confusingly, no. 10 Kingsdown Parade.
41. Nos 37-40 Somerset Street.
42. Ashley House (14 Somerset Street).
43. No. 10 Kingdown Parade.
44. It continued providing accommodation for similar social services—in an increasingly sorry state of disrepair—until finally, in 1984, Avon County Council decided it was 'surplus to requirements'. The house was sold and converted into seven private flats.
45. No. 3 King Square. Latimer, *op. cit.*, vol. 3, pp.199 and 475.
46. No. 1 King Square.

47. No. 27 King Square. Latimer, *op. cit.*, vol. 3, p.477.
48. Coe Church and McPherson (Comac), nos 16-23 King Square.
49. First no. 15, then nos 13 and 14 King Square. They currently occupy nos 1, 14, 15 and 24 King Square.
50. W.M. Llewellin died 1930.
51. Patricia Hollis, *Ladies Elect: Women in English Local Government 1865-1914*, 1987 and June Hannam, 'An Enlarged Sphere of Usefulness: The Bristol's Women's Movement *c.*1860-1914' in *The Making of Modern Bristol*, ed. Madge Dresser and Philip Ollerenshaw, 1996.
52. Emily (1847-92), Helen (1858-1945) and Elizabeth (1849-1944) Sturge, part of a family of 11 children, lived at no. 25 Somerset Street in the 1850s and '60s, before moving from Kingsdown in 1864. Mary Clifford (1842-1919) lived first at no. 8 and then at no. 26 Somerset Street from 1842-54.
53. No. 2 Apsley Villas.
54. At no. 10 Kingsdown Parade.
55. T. Greenwood, *Public Libraries, their organisation, uses and management*, 1890.
56. Resident at no. 66 Kingsdown Parade. Arrowsmith, *Dictionary of Bristol*, 1884.
57. *Bristol Mirror*, 15 January 1853.
58. The *Western Daily Press*, 16 June 1880, reported that a match between the Kingsdown and Leander swimming clubs had been held there.
59. H.E. Meller, *Leisure and the Changing City*, 1870-1914, p.231.
60. Bishop's Committee report, 1884.

FOUR *War and Peace*

1. On the site of the previous Truant School.
2. St James was closed when its site came within the hospital zone in the 1960s. St Michael's still flourishes.
3. Charles Harvey and Jon Press, *Sir George White of Bristol*, 1989; Sir George White, *Tramlines to the Stars*, 1995.
4. No. 18 Kingsdown Parade.
5. The shop was there from 1906-65.
6. Nos 33-51 Kingsdown Parade.
7. Bristol District Laundry bought nos 23 and 24 St Matthew's Road in 1930 and no. 25 in 1933.
8. In all some 3,840 children were evacuated to Britain. The children, together with 120 helpers, 15 Catholic priests and two doctors, sailed for Southampton in May 1937. By mid-September, thanks to various religious and political establishments, they had all been rehoused in 94 'colonies' situated all around the country.
9. At 52 Kingsdown Parade. Correspondence with later occupants of the lodgings. The landlady commented that 'whilst Powell was nice enough, Nunn May was very deep'.
10. Portway House (no. 26 St Matthew's Road).
11. *Western Daily Press*, 30 May 1941.
12. No. 10 Kingsdown Parade, 16a Kingsdown Parade.
13. The heavy brass cannons standing outside the fort sailed over the houses to land in the garden of no. 10 Kingsdown Parade.
14. Now the site of Priors Hill Flats.
15. The acre of land bounded by Alfred Place, Southwell Street and Walker Street.
16. There are now 208 listed buildings in Kingsdown, though this increase is in part due to a change in the official definition. Before 1967 only individual houses could be listed for their architectural or historic merit; since then an area can be listed because of the value of the whole group.
17. *Western Daily Press*, December 1956.
18. One of the founder members of the Association was the formidable Mrs Amy Geaney

of Somerset Street, whose splendid collection of press cuttings of those tumultuous years has proved an invaluable research source.

19. *Western Daily Press*, 24 September 1958.
20. *Manchester Guardian*, 17 January 1959.
21. *Observer*, 19 January 1959.
22. *Gloucester Countryside*, 1957.
23. *Observer*, 19 January 1959.
24. *Bristol Civic News*, no. 122, July/August 1968.
25. The Kingsdown boundary runs north along the western end of the 1912 King Edward Building.
26. The first visible sign of development was the new boiler house in Southwell Street completed in 1957, providing heat to all existing and future hospital buildings through distribution tunnels. Twenty-seven dirty and inefficient coal-fired boiler houses were closed resulting in almost total elimination of smoke and considerable cost benefit to the hospital authorities. However, a large chimney now towered over Kingsdown and there were many complaints about pollution from it.
27. From 1963-92 the building housed the Bristol Technical College (later known as Brunel College of Technology) and since then it has become part of the University of Bristol Pre-Clinical Veterinary School.

FIVE   *The Late 20th and Early 21st Centuries*

1. The original Conservation Area—more or less bounded by Kingsdown Parade to the north and Dove Street to the south, from Alfred Place in the west to Springfield Road in the east—was expanded at the south-west corner as far as Alfred Hill in 1977; and that corner was further extended to Horfield Road in 2008.
2. Whicheloe Macfarlane working with the JT Building Group.
3. Ryan McKee Architects. The paddock (with resident horse removed for the night) was used for many years for the local Guy Fawkes celebrations. Across the road the six end houses of Alfred Place terrace, blitzed in the war, were reinstated in replica as housing association flats in 1982 by architects Moxley Jenner.
4. Modus were the architects for the first scheme, Percy Thomas for the second.
5. Including nos 24, 26, 28 Marlborough Hill, 40 Alfred Hill, 4 Cottage Place and nos 78-84 Horfield Rd.
6. No. 17 Marlborough Hill.
7. *Evening Post*, 9 July 1986.
8. The ex-Barrow Hospital land.
9. Inscape Architects.
10. A planning application the following year to turn it into offices was rejected, following co-ordinated objection led by a Kingsdown resident. Finally, in 1993, an eminently suitable application was approved for the Roman Catholic 'Little Brothers of Nazareth', who care for the homeless. Later they expanded to run the St James Priory Project from the church and adjoining buildings, providing support for those with substance dependency, a use that continues to the present day.

Bibliography

Primary Sources

Title deeds and documents in Bristol Record Office:

BRO 18387	
BRO 40101	
BRO 6098	Three deeds relating to the *Montague Hotel*.
BRO 3810	House next to the *Montague Hotel*, 1776.
BRO 21782/115/A	Prior's Hill, fee farm rents 1694-1741.
BRO 207679	Hillgrove Street, conveyance of land, 1737.
BRO 4628	Nos 8 and 9 Southwell Street, 1739.
BRO 11054(62)	No. 17 King Square, 1753.
BRO 12527(26)	House in King Square, 1758.
BRO 32005(1-5)	Dighton Street, 1753-63.
BRO 29571(3)	Duke Street, record of landownership, pre-1759.
BRO 29571(2)	Charles Street (Brickhouse Lane), 1780.
BRO 35194(1-37)	Nos 1 and 2 Somerset Street, 1787.
BRO 18876(1-26)	Nos 23-5 St Matthew's Road.
BRO 03457(1-3)	No. 10 Kingsdown Parade.
BRO 18609(14-16c)	No. 18 Kingsdown Parade.
BRO 40563(1-10)	No. 58 Kingsdown Parade.
BRO 40648	Deeds of Nos 64 and 66 Kingsdown Parade, 1792-
BRO 4965(a-b)	1809, showing delay in completion of building.
BRO 38601(1-12)	No. 74 Kingsdown Parade.
BRO 17132(1-4)	No. 78 Kingsdown Parade.
BRO 26138(1-18)	No. 79 Kingsdown Parade.
BRO 35447	St Matthew's Church building contract, 1833.
BRO 39400(1-2)	Bankruptcy papers, *c.*1837, re. Thomas Gay Ransford, who owned property in Somerset Street.

Latimer, J., 'A Deed Relating to the Partition of the Property of St James, Bristol', Proceedings of the Clifton Antiquarian Club, 1898.

Parish Documents in Bristol Record Office

P/StJ/HM/1	Grant of Priory and its possessions to Henry Brayne, 1544.
P/StJ/HM/4(a-h)	The Rev. F.W. Potto-Hicks, unpublished MA thesis on St James's Church, undated.
P/StJ/ChW/6	Perambulation of parish boundaries, 1751.
P/StJ/OP/1/(1-20)	Poor Rate Records, 17th century.

P/StJ/V/I/4   Transcript of Vestry Book, 1659-91.
P/StJ/D/6 and D/14/1-2   Deeds relating to the Dighton family.

Books and Pamphlets

Arrowsmith, J.W. and Spear, H.J. (eds.), Arrowsmith's *Dictionary of Bristol*, Bristol, 1884

Barrett, Wm., *The History and Antiquities of the City of Bristol*, Alan Sutton, Gloucester, 1982, reprint of 1789 publication.

Brace, Keith, *Portrait of Bristol*, Robert Hale, London, 1971

Brierley, L. and Reid, H., *Go Home and do the Washing!*, Broadcast Books, Bristol, 2000

Charlton, J. and Milton, P.M., *Redland 791-1800*, Bristol, 1851

Dresser, M. and Ollerenshaw, P. (eds.), *The Making of Modern Bristol*, Redcliffe Press, 1996

Dresser, Madge, *Slavery Obscured*, Continuum, London and New York, 2001

De Gomme, B. (eds. Firth, C. and Leslie, J.H.), 'The Siege and Capture of Bristol by the Royalist Forces in 1643', *Journal of Historical Research*, vol. 4

Evans, John, *A Chronological Outline of the History of Bristol and Stranger's Guide through its Streets and Neighbourhood*, Bristol, 1824

Frankcom, G. and Musgrave, J.H., *The Irish Giant*, Duckworth & Co., London 1976

Gibson, Cyril, *The Bristol School Board, 1871-1903*, Bristol Branch of the Historical Association, 1997

Gomme, Andor, Jenner, Michael and Little, Bryan, *Bristol, An Architectural History*, Lund Humphries, London, 1979

Hall, I.V., 'Whitsun Sugar House', *Transactions of Bristol and Gloucestershire Archaeological Society*, vol. 65, pp.1-97

Hardiman, S., *The 1832 Cholera Epidemic and its Impact on the City of Bristol*, Bristol Branch of the Historical Association, 2005

Harding, J., *Bristol Charters, 1155-1373*, Bristol Record Society, vol. 1, 1930

Harding, S. and Lambert, D., *Parks and Gardens of Avon*, Avon Gardens Trust, 1994

Harvey, Charles and Press, Jon, *Sir George White of Bristol*, Bristol Branch of the Historical Association, 1989

Hicks, Margery, *Young Yesterday*, Wordens of Cornwall, Penzance, 1969

Hutton, Stanley, *Bristol and its Famous Associations*, Arrowsmith, Bristol, 1907

Ison, Walter, *The Georgian Buildings of Bristol*, Kingsmead Press, Bath, reprint 1978

Ivamy, E.R. Hardy (ed.), *Mozeley and Whitely's Law Dictionary*, Butterworths, London, 1988

Jackson, Edward, *A Study in Democracy: Industrial Co-operation in Bristol*, Manchester, 1911

Jackson, Reg et al, *Excavations at St.James's Priory, Bristol*, Oxbow Books, 2006

Lambert, A.J., *The Chapel on the Hill*, St Stephen's Press, 1929

Large, D. and Round, F., *Public Health in the Mid-Victorian Bristol*, Bristol Branch of the Historical Association, 1974

Latimer, J., *The Annals of Bristol in the Eighteenth Century*, Bristol, 1893

Leech, Roger, *The St Michael's Hill Precinct of the University of Bristol*, Bristol Branch of the Historical Association, 2000

Lynch, John, *For King and Parliament: Bristol and the Civil War*, Sutton Publishing, Stroud, 1999

McGrath, Patrick, *Bristol and the Civil War*, Bristol Branch of the Historical Association, 1981

Mayo, Ronald, *The Huguenots in Bristol*, Bristol Branch of the Historical Association, 1985

Mellor, H.E., *Leisure and the Changing City, 1870-1914*, Routledge and Kegan Paul, 1976

Mellor, P., *A Kingsdown Community*, Bristol, 1985.

Mellor, P., *A Kingsdown Collection*, Bristol, 1987

Nabb, Harold, *The Bristol Gas Industry, 1815-1949*, Bristol Branch of the Historical Association, 1987

Neale, Frances, 'William Worcester: the Topography of Medieval Bristol', transcription published by Bristol Record Society, vol. 51, 2000

Nicholls, J.F. and Taylor, John, *Bristol Past and Present*, 3 vols., London and Bristol, 1881

Oliver, George, *Collections Illustrating the History of the Catholic Religion in Cornwall, Devon, Dorset, Somerset, Wiltshire and Gloucestershire*, Chas. Dolman, London, 1857

Ponsford, M.W., *Excavations at Greyfriars, Bristol*, City of Bristol Museum and Art Gallery, 1975

Priest, G. and Cobb, P. (eds.), *The Fight for Bristol*, Bristol Civic Society and Redcliffe Press, 1980

Punter, John, *Design Control in Bristol, 1940-1990*, Redcliffe Press, 1990

Ralph, E. and Williams, M.E., 'Inhabitants of Bristol, 1696', Bristol Record Society, vol. XXV, 1968

Richardson, David, *Bristol, Africa and the Eighteenth-Century Slave Trade to America*, 4 vols., Bristol Record Society, vol. 1 no. 37 (1986), vol. 2 no. 39 (1987), vol. 3 no. 42 (1991) and vol. 4 no. 47 (1996)

Russell, James, *The Civil War Defences of Bristol: their Archaeology and Topography*, Bristol, 2nd edition, 2003

Seyer, Samuel, *Memoirs Historical and Topographical of Bristol and its Neighbourhood*, vols. 1 and 2, Bristol, 1823

Sturge, C., *Some Little Quakers in their Nursery*, J. Batler, Bristol, 1829

Sturge, E., *Reminiscences of my Life*, Arrowsmith, Bristol, 1828

Tate, W.E., *The Parish Chest*, Cambridge United Press, 1960

White, George, *Tramlines to the Stars*, Redcliffe Press, 1995

Williams, G.M., *Mary Clifford*, Arrowsmith, Bristol, 1920

Unpublished Source

Leech, Roger, 'An Archaeological Desktop Evaluation of no. 6 Kingsdown Parade and adjacent properties for the United Bristol Healthcare NHS Trust', 1998

Index

(a page number in bold denotes an illustration)

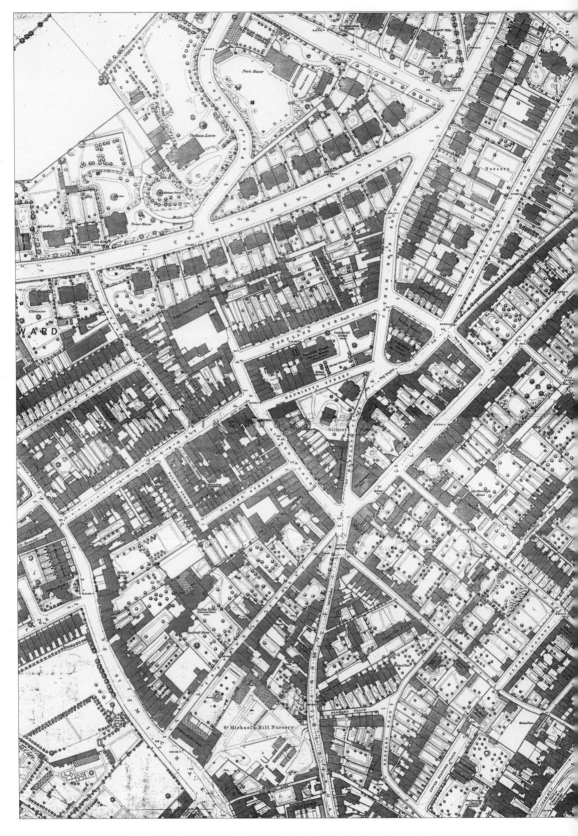

From the 1st edition Ordnance Survey 1885 (sections LXXI.16.9, 10, 14 and 15)